MAIDEN MAGICK

A TEEN'S GUIDE TO GODDESS WISDOM AND RITUAL

by

C.C.Brondwin

NEW PAGE BOOKS
A division of The Career Press, Inc.
Franklin Lakes, NJ

MAIDEN MAGICK
EDITED BY KATE HENCHES
TYPESET BY EILEEN DOW MUNSON
Cover design and illustrations by Christine Ahmad
Printed in the U.S.A. by Book-mart Press

To order this title, please call toll-free 1-800-CAREER-1 (NJ and Canada: 201-848-0310) to order using VISA or MasterCard, or for further information on books from Career Press.

The Career Press, Inc., 3 Tice Road, PO Box 687,
Franklin Lakes, NJ 07417
www.careerpress.com
www.newpagebooks.com

Library of Congress Cataloging-in-Publication Data

Brondwin, C. C., 1945-
    Maiden magick : a teens guide to Goddess wisdom and ritual / C.C. Brondwin.
    p. cm.
Includes bibliographical references and index.
ISBN 1-56414-670-7 (pbk.)
    1. Magic, Celtic. 2. Mythology, Celtic. 3. Goddess religion. 4. Ritual. I. Title.

BF1622.C45B76 2003
299—dc21
                                                                    2002045246

dedication

With love for
Emma Hendry Caron, my goddess-daughter
and
Anna Gerrard, friend of the faeries

and, as always,
for my beloved
William D. Johnson

acknowledgments

Inspiration and encouragement for this book came from many sources. I send my heartfelt appreciation to those from the Otherworld who helped me: the Clan Mothers who whispered their ancient wisdom; my spirit guides; my guardians; and all my ancestors who were steadfast in their advice and love.

And to those here on Abred, I offer bushels of fond appreciation to: my favorite and only brother, **Herb Swinhoe,** for the insights he shared from his years of work with teens and, too, for instilling in me, from my childhood days, the belief that I could achieve anything; **Michael Chapman,** for his valuable direction for this book that came from his humanitarian work and his long service as a much-loved counselor to youth; **Francyne Laliberte,** for her thoughtful and much-appreciated gifts, and for the bountiful love she shares through her artistry with natural foods; **Gerrard and Cath McKay,** a special thanks for their overwhelming generosity that saw us safely through the dark side of our moon; **Maureen Hendry,** an old-soul friend who walks Abred and the dreamworld with the ease of a Celtic shaman; **Kelly Moon,** for the safe shelter of her magickal cottage where I wrote happily in the daily company of her ancestral spirits; **Mary**

Hunter, her Auntie, and a true Clan Mother, who inspires and gently pushes me when I need it; **Eroca Ryon,** for her undying faith in the success of my work and for sharing her enchanted brand of healing magick; **Elizabeth Ferguson,** who holds my hand tightly as we walk together in the same direction but on different paths, Hai-Hai; **Gillian Browning and Sahana**, keepers and healers of the horse spirits; **Sue Stanger,** who happily sails down the Goddess path with a joyful, caring, and compassionate spirit; **Judy Brown,** for her constant encouragement, wry observations, and ready laugh; **Gloria Jensen,** my fisher-friend, for cheering me on and buoying my faith in myself; **Alison Diakiw**, my sister-friend and supporter, who endured a long healing journey with Goddess courage, and triumphed; my excellent healers on Abred, **Dr. Marc Puts, Dr. Steven Edworthy,** and **Elisia Teixeria,** who cheerfully moved mountains for me; my amazing and accomplished niece **Kelly Ferris,** who showed me that Celtic Aunties still have a welcome role to play in young women's lives; **Joanne Cherry**, and **Katya Karpenko**, long-time friends who have always been there for me through the many jolting bumps and dangerous curves of the incredible journey we've shared; **Christine Ahmad,** for her delightful illustrations of this book and my last, *The Clan of the Goddess*, (New Page Books); my children, **Jay Johnson,** my son, for his joyful approach to life and for the loving gift of truly believing in me; **Linda Johnson**, his wife, a dedicated healer; **Melissa Johnson Mitchell,** my daughter, a soul-star who never fails to brighten darkened skies, and her kind and loving husband, **Scot Mitchell**; and, of course, to that vast and talented band of rogues, artists, and comedians, I'm honored to call my dear friends who so readily applaud my every accomplishment and thrill my heart with non-stop laughter; the terrific **Staff** at **New Page Books,** for their warm professionalism; and, as always, to my personal editor and the love-of-my-life, the unflappable **Billy Johnson**.

Contents

The Aunties Welcome You

Hello there! We've been waiting for you. Come over here and don't be shy. 'Tis a dark and lonely night, but 'tis safe and comfy by our campfire.

See who's sitting round the crackling fire? Why, 'tis none other than your very own Clan Mothers, those ancient Celts of the Goddess Clan. Aye, they're called your loving Aunties and they're here to bid you welcome. Go ahead. Seat yourself on that log over there, close by the fire, and take this warm bear pelt to pull over your chilled shoulders.

Listen now...your Aunties are spinning tales about women's magick, about warrior queens, faeries, and kindly spirits from the Otherworld. They speak of strong, admirable women who practice the Goddess arts. Ah, I've heard all these ancient legends before but...wait...there's something else....

Ha! Hear that? Now they're talking about a gifted maiden full of promise and wondrous, healing magick. Well, I'll be! They're talking about *you*.

Aye, that they are. They are speaking about you and all that you may become when you choose to walk softly, yet proudly, beside them on the Goddess Path. They know about your beautiful story, about your great lifelong adventure, about your spiritual possibilities, about your natural magick, and all about your promising future.

Hurry. Read on and see what they have to say in this wee book about finding your way along the Goddess Path. Don't miss a single word because your Aunties will reveal all the steps you need to follow to begin your spiritual journey into the amazing world of spirits and loving guardians.

If you choose to come along, this will surely be an awesome journey of spiritual apprenticeship.

Are you game?

Good girl!

Then let's not waste one nanosecond.

Let's go, Magick Maiden...

ENTER.

Part One

The Comfort of Belonging

CHAPTER 1

A Big Cosmic Hug

Hey! Listen up...here's the Goddess truth:

YOU ARE AMAZING. YOU ARE DIVINE.

Don't shake your head. It is a fact. And what's more, you'd better get used to hearing this beautiful truth about yourself.

As if.

No, listen. It's true. The women of the Goddess believe in you. They love and respect you. But the best news of all is that you, by birth, can rightfully claim membership in this magickal age-old spiritual sisterhood. The feminine essence lives in your heart, in your soul. You are not just any teen wandering about, feeling like maybe you don't belong—oh, no—you are an essential and beloved part of the timeless sisterhood of "knowing" women, this enduring cosmic circle of Goddess love.

Admit it. There is nothing we women enjoy more than the kindly companionship of kindred spirits. It's true, isn't it? It is a great and comforting feeling to be among fine friends and fellow travelers who understand us. Who appreciate us. Who don't put us down. Ah…that's a bit of heaven—or a bit of Avalon, as the old Wisewomen, the Clan Mothers, would say. You've experienced it—call it a rush, or a bit of sweet happiness, or a burst of joy. Belonging is truly beautiful.

Yes, my young Spiritual Seeker, by feeling the rush of wild curiosity that has you reading these lines, you lay claim to your woman's ancestral right to lifetime membership in this ancient sisterhood of the Goddess in which women practice their magick for the good of all, and help other women to grow and thrive— to jump and jive! Belonging to the great kinship of women of the Goddess is your woman's birthright, yet it is long forgotten.

Now, before we go one baby-step further, let me make a pledge. I know that, as a teenager, you often feel marginalized, misunderstood, and discouraged when dealing with the "adult" world. So clearly understand that *I respectfully consider you to be "of age."* You are not a silly, unfocused "teen" or a young woman hopelessly adrift in life—no way! In truth, you deserve to be encouraged and applauded.

In my Celtic ancestry, as in many other societies, maidens were initiated as full apprentices into the spiritual and intellectual life of their clans, or tribes, or communities at your very age. Young women, just like you, were considered capable, responsible, and ready for the deep and meaningful work of spiritual discovery. So be clear on this:

I CONSIDER YOU TO BE A WONDROUS AND REMARKABLE SPIRITUAL WOMAN IN THE MAKING—A STRONG AND COURAGEOUS SPIRIT UNFOLDING. I RESPECT YOUR INTELLIGENCE, YOUR DEVELOPING ABILITIES, YOUR NATURAL MAGICKAL TALENTS, AND YOUR CREATIVE NATURE. I AM HONORED TO MEET YOU. CALL ME AUNT C.C., AND I'LL CALL YOU AMAZING.

I come from a family of Celtic healers, soothsayers, and mystics, so my experience and advice to you is based on this ethnic and spiritual background. It is part and parcel of who I am, and it is the place from which I can speak my truth. But the Goddess truly belongs to everyone: She is all nationalities, all accents, all colors, all loving. She is part of the great complexity that forms your nature and defines your whole self. She belongs to you and guides you. You and the Goddess force are one.

It seems hard to believe that long ago in this structured place we call Abred, or Earth, teenagers had such high value. But to early Celtic tribes, they did indeed. Tribal Elders, called the Clan Mothers, as well as all the other adults in the clan, pledged their faith and tradition to help maidens find their way in life, and to assist them with their spiritual journey whenever possible. As an apprentice, you could have called on beloved Elders, and other specially talented or skilled adults, to help you with your career or training choices; to unravel your latest baffling boyfriend troubles; or to listen to your innermost concerns regarding your place in this world and in the next. When you approached an Elder, they'd willingly advise you based on their own experience. In turn, when you grew older and wiser, you'd do the same for the next generation of young Spiritual Seekers.

It was as simple as that. As a teen girl in the tribe, as a Celtic maiden, you were considered a most valuable and beloved resource. And it made sense. The Celts realized that it was you and your friends who would ensure a rich cultural and spiritual life for the healthy continuance of the Clan. You were their lifeblood, their faith, their only hope for the future. That is still an essential truth. Unfortunately, today's community leaders often forget or offhandedly dismiss the importance of your role in their big fat tomorrows. What a shame. What a sad and foolish loss. But that shouldn't stop you from standing up and speaking out. No way!

So, what was life like in those Celtic Clan days? Well, a Celtic maiden's world was rich and magickal. It was filled with hard learning, intensive ritual and meaningful ceremonies; but it was also made lively with wild dances around blazing camp-fires with dear friends and handsome, playful lovers. It was demanding, yet soul-satisfying, for you had a strong, clear voice they took the time to listen to, and you brought fresh, inventive ideas to be duly considered by the Clan. Hard work, hard play, and high status in the community would have marked your days among the early Celts.

Being valued and being listened to—even with a dash of hard work—sounds appealing, doesn't it? It might even make you long for those ancient Celtic times when everyone followed the feminine Divine, the Great Mother. A time when magick, spells, and talking to the spirits or faeries were everyday happenings. I, for one, would love to slip out of my skin and go back there to mix up healing herbs, or make potions for the lovesick, or cast a group spell to prevent a war...Say, if you came along with me, we'd have a blast! So...Could we go?

Well, no, we can't. But, then again...*yes*, we can. Confused? Let's do the math.

First and foremost, you and I were born in the "here and now" for a very definite reason. You, my courageous friend, have valuable work to do on planet Earth. Yes, you do. You came into this life gifted by the Goddess with specific talents that no one else was granted, that no one can ever steal from you or even copy. You are one of a kind. A beautiful work of art in progress.

And, most likely, you chose to be born at this very time—to your very own family—for a zillion and one different reasons. I know at times that's hard to believe when family life is stressful but, admit it: There are other times when you are truly glad to be in your particular family and in this very familiar place called the "here and now." Am I right?

It is essential on your spiritual voyage not to lose the sense of time and place you chose to be born into; it is also important to explore fully the extent of your numinous, spiritual self and your magical roots while staying grounded in the present. If you remain firmly planted on Abred—feet on the ground and keenly aware of life around you—then, Spiritual Seeker, your spirit will soar.

All clear so far? We're in the "here and now," even if a part of us longs to be elsewhere.

Now, let's discuss the complicated "yes" part about your spirit going back in time. You *can* enjoy the benefits of those ancient times because—stick with me, I want you to bend your mind a little—you are not *entirely* of this world.

Yikes! How so, C.C.?

Well, the Celts believed that you live with "one foot in each world." That is, with one foot firmly planted on the Earth plane, Abred; and one foot in the spiritual realm, often called the Otherworld. And they lived that way, every day. They were part human, part divine, just as you are. They had their jobs—crops to put in, yarn to spin, babies to birth—yet they also enjoyed the whimsical company of the spirits, the support of their distant ancestors, the thrill of the faerie folk and the often-invisible little people who populated their lives. Their faith encompassed both the wonders of Nature and the luminous mists of the dream state, the active imagination or the beyond.

The line between the two planes (Abred and the Otherworld) was often blurry. They said of themselves that they lived "betwixt and between" the two worlds. They lived their magick every day and so can you. By cocking your ear to the inner self, by tuning in to the coaching and coaxing of your loving supportive Goddess force, you too will be well on your way to discovering your deep soul work, your real work, your beloved work.

The maidens of the Clan were fortunate to enjoy a rich duality of the spirit and imagination. It offered a joyous detour from life's humdrum days, and a fine refuge in anxious or bummed-out times. Life may have been hard among the medieval tribes scrambling for survival—as your own life can sometimes be, right?—but it was a magickal way of life and, to tell the truth, it was a bit of a high.

Young Celtic maidens were taught that the Goddess wasn't just out there somewhere, above them or below them…or whatever. No way. Nothing that separate or disenfranchised. The Goddess is an integral part of you. She is you. You are She. Where do you find Her? She dwells within your mind, your heart, and your very soul. She supports and encourages you. She is your very best friend and your greatest ally, and She remains so today. Though persecutions in the Middle Ages forced Her to dwell in secrecy for a long cold time, She never stopped empowering Earthly women, never gave up on them. She is re-born in every female child's soul, and in the feminine side of every male child. Her presence is timeless, enduring, and needed.

Hey! Here's the exciting part. You are on the brink of making spiritual history; trend setting; trail-blazing. Why? Because you were born into the exact time in history that will be known as the Re-awakening of the Goddess. You, my friend, are smack in the center of all that is magickal; all that is truly meaningful. You stand ready to throw open the cosmic door in greeting and say: "Where have you been Goddess-mine?" And you will serve to change the world for the better for all your sisters, now and to come.

What's in it for you? Hey, it's okay to ask. What will the Goddess willingly do for you and the development of your life?

A lot. More than you can imagine, I promise. The Goddess Force of Good will unleash the full range of your amazing possibilities. She'll help activate your dormant and unique magickal powers. She'll give you back your innate sense of self-knowledge and show you your real life purpose. She'll help raise your awareness to go out in the world and demand greater social justice, tolerance, and global understanding. With Her at your side, you'll stand up and be counted; you'll speak out; you'll wrestle the unkind and the small-spirited out of your way.

We Celts call Her your "Help Meet" and She will *help you meet* up to your full potential as the tough, complicated, creative, sensitive, and oh-so-capable young woman you really are. She'll nudge you into action, and She will laugh and holler out loud with you on this most groovy and exciting spiritual adventure called your life's journey.

You'll be surprised to learn that some things don't change. Today, you are a mirror image of the young Clanswomen I talk about. At your core, you are a naturally wild and beautiful creature, tough and strong and determined, yet willing and able to dance lightly "betwixt and between" both worlds. This is your elemental magick; your unique woman's magick; your Goddess magick; your Maiden Magick. Following the Goddess Path, living your own truth, is an empowering, thrilling, not-to-be-missed experience. Want to go for it? Are you nodding? Yes?

Hey, great decision! Congratulations, you Spiritual Seeker.

The Goddess kisses your beautiful face.

She hugs you.

She dances you around the room.

You do belong.

Blessed, blessed be.

The Straight Story—
Tell Me No Lies

What does it **really** mean to walk the Path of the Goddess?

Be advised, Spiritual Seeker: There is deep soul work set out before you. You must agree in your heart to make a personal commitment—one of the most serious ones you'll ever make—for this single principle will forever guide your steps:

TO BELIEVE IN THE GODDESS IS TO BELIEVE IN YOURSELF.

It is such a simple concept, yet it is incredibly challenging.

Your assignment, should you choose to accept it:

You must decide to let go of your lesser self. You will pledge to make a sincere effort to cast off the negative aspects of a your teen life until now, to cast away the things that drag you down and erode your soul or endanger your self-esteem. Wave good-bye forever to your many insecurities, your pettiness, your past hurts, your needless guilt, your unkind ways, and your lack of faith in yourself. Out with all that useless psychic garbage! You are about to re-create yourself as a strong, spiritual woman who is sure of herself, relaxed, attractive in her self-assurance, and loads of good fun to be with. That young woman of virtue, of kindness, of deep-down strength is—you!

Wait. There's more.

Your heartfelt commitment is based on the values of clanswomen who practiced the Old Ways in all corners of the Earth. Here is your homework. To fully walk the Goddess Path you must honestly acknowledge and accept:

- That you have major worth and value in this world.
- That you will stand tall and sure of yourself.
- That you will develop your gift of women's intuition and your own brand of helpful magick.
- That you will stand up for the downtrodden or those unfairly treated.
- That you will actively protect the environment that is the body of the Great Mother.
- That you will accumulate as much training, education, and skills as are possible.
- That you will honor the creative side of your nature and develop it with confidence.
- That you will love with deep emotion and playful enjoyment.
- That you will always remember to laugh at yourself.
- That you will enjoy all the pleasures Abred has to offer while you are here.

Not candy fluff—this Goddess commitment—is it? Remember, you've come to this place as a Spiritual Seeker, looking for your own brand of women's magick and for the better way.

Are you a maiden with great magickal potential? Yes, you nod, *"I think so."*

Then come along. Let's embrace all the wonders and satisfaction of walking the Goddess Path.

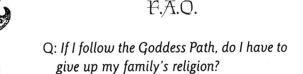

F.A.Q.

Q: If I follow the Goddess Path, do I have to give up my family's religion?

A: Not unless that is your choice. Be clear on this: To know the Goddess is to live and practice what She teaches, and to recognize Her feminine spirit within your own soul. It is not a formal religion with long lists of do's and don'ts and horrific punishments if you color outside the lines. The Goddess is and always has been a tolerant, loving presence.

In fact, the Goddess Path is followed by many women closely associated with organized religion. There are news stories every day about nuns who have prayer groups devoted to Her, or women within established religions who organize women's healing circles and make room for the Goddess in their homes and hearts. They don't give up their original faith, so why should you? Women's faith in the Goddess is everywhere, growing each and every day. It is a quiet revolution of thinking and believing, often referred to as the Women's Spirituality Movement, but it has no headquarters or anointed leaders. Most importantly, it is happening within women's hearts.

So go ahead, Magickal Maiden, explore the ancient sisterhood of the Goddess but don't abandon your traditional religious training. Enjoy it all. The Great Mother wants you to grow and expand, not narrow down or diminish yourself in any way. Just remember, to follow the Goddess is to know and respect Her through the way you live your life, through the attitudes you have and through the good brand of women's magick and healing you practice. Believing that the Goddess lives within naturally encourages a woman to live life to its fullest potential. Now, that's a fine thing.

chapter 2

Surprise! Your Spiritual Teacher Has Arrived

The Clan Mothers taught that music and books can relay strong messages directly to your soul, to answer your spirit's burning questions, or to satisfy the heart's deep longings. I know you've experienced that tingling feeling when you hear a certain tune that reminds you of someone you love. Maybe the hair stands up on your arms, or you shiver from the sharp sensation of the memory. This is especially true with old boyfriends, right? Those sappy, romantic songs you heard when the two of you were together can bring it all back in a flash. Drat. But music is and always has been a sacred tool of the ancient craft of remembering.

Well, there are other cosmic tools that often bring someone or something—such as a message from the Otherworld—to you. The Clan Mothers believed that spiritual help is always close at hand and when the apprentice—that's you—is ready and eager to learn, the teacher will appear.

Teachers come to us in many forms answering to our needs. Some will travel long distances with you along your Path; others will walk only a short way, holding your hand and helping you to avoid life's sudden potholes and mud puddles, all the while whispering their particular wisdom in your ear and sharing a laugh or two.

Often your spiritual teacher will be a person, but not always. It could be a particularly significant course at school that fires you up and makes you rethink everything in your life. Sometimes it will be a group of like-minded people who join you to walk a little way down your collective path before veering off in their own directions. Or it can be a very special book that seems written just for you.

Bingo! That's it.

This book, *Maiden Magick*, is your omen—a portent of coming growth and certain change. You seem intent on this spiritual adventure and (at the risk of appearing immodest) it looks as though you just may have some agreeable company— me (C.C. Brondwin), author of this book and your teacher of the moment.

Pretty bold of me, don't you think? Hey, the Goddess loves women to be brash and bold and sure of themselves. But *"Who the heck are you, and how do you know so much?"* you rightly ask. Good question. Read the following section called "Why C.C. is your Appointed Guide." You see, helping you along your Path of inner discovery is simply part of my women's spiritual legacy. So, you clever teen goddess, if you read on it looks like you've accepted me as your spiritual mentor for a short while, and you are willing to become my Apprentice. This wee book is your tour guide for extreme goddess adventure. What a roller coaster of fun and wonder lies ahead for us!

And you deserve hearty, back-slapping praise for opening the book and reading this far. Well done! Why? Because, clearly, you have correctly interpreted a cosmic sign—this little book—left scattered across your life Path by those Wisewomen of the Celtic Clans. Just think, by the simple act of reading the following chapters, you'll develop your own brand of Maiden Magick; expand your instinctive understanding of the Goddess; transform your everyday social interactions; open your heart to more love and happiness; and, all the while, you'll be following in the footsteps of the great and noble Clan Mothers of yesteryear who gladly light your way. Are you up for it?

Good girl! I can see that you've accepted the challenge with the admirable grace of a developing goddess and that rocks!

Take my hand and I'll introduce you to this Goddess Clan, this community of women that spans time and space. I'll do my best to teach you the ancient magick and I sense that you, in turn, will return the favor and teach me something cool and exciting.

Why C.C. Is Your Appointed Guide

The answer is simple: Because my mother told me to be.

That's right, I may be a crone, but I still do what my mother tells me—at least when it comes to spiritual matters. You see, my mom was my spiritual teacher, as was my grandmother and, later, my Irish mother-in-law. They were some of my Clan Mothers and though they are all in Avalon (heaven) now, they still guide me and often come to remind me of who I am and what I'm supposed to be doing here on Abred.

I was raised in a household of mystics, healers, and natural channelers that made *Buffy the Vampire Slayer*, or the old TV show *I Dream of Jeannie* seem like an after-school visit to my house. There were so many talismans and charms adorning me that I sounded like a one-woman band when I walked. I had a rabbit's foot in my pocket, lucky silver coins sewn into the hem of my heavy winter coats, and so many energy-charged stones in my jeans that I limped. I wore herbs in red fabric envelopes beneath my undershirt, and, during the cold Winter months, I had so many cloves of fresh garlic hanging in muslin pouches that I could have stopped in my tracks and whipped up a killer Caesar salad for you, any time, any place.

Every weekend we'd have a family séance to conjure up spirits and guides, and even important public figures such as Winston Churchill. I was cautioned never to tell anyone because they may think I was, well, a little "weird," but I couldn't wait to get outside and broadcast it to the entire neighborhood.

By high school I knew everything—no, I really did. All the hidden things. Like what? Well, my mother would say before a school dance: *"Watch for the boy with the green eyes in the blue button-down shirt. He's in love with you and…you are going to break his heart."* Yikes! As things unfolded, she was right-on. Or she'd warn: *"Whatever you do, promise me that you won't ride in that old red beater car tonight."* That was a more serious warning, for three friends were in a serious car accident that night in—you guessed it—the red car.

It wasn't long before friends said: *"Ask your mother about that, would ya?"* She'd talk to them about their boyfriends, or a friend's betrayal, or some fresh heartbreak. My Celtic Mom was cool. All my friends were drawn to her. She was a true Clan Mother. She always made time for my friends—reading their fortunes with tea leaves or cards and always teasing them—my kitchen used to ring with laughter. High school was a blast! Oh, don't worry, I stopped wearing the garlic after grade five.

But then I got serious, had a career in advertising, television, and radio, and eventually I was a stuffy bigwig in universities. Still, I made some bad choices in men, took wrong turns, and suffered all the other yucky mistakes we women need to experience in order to mature and open our hearts to real compassion and understanding. Finally, a serious illness slammed me into bed for a good long time. I began to research and study and come back to my natural birthright—the one we share—full membership in the timeless Goddess Clan.

Because I am a writer, I am guided to connect with you this way, and it looks as if you have chosen me to be your guide along this part of your long and winding spiritual Path. I am so pleased.

A Spell to Draw the Love of the Clan Mothers

This is a quick feel-good spell that lets you experience the warmth, comfort, and all-abiding love of your Clan Mothers. I promise that you are totally safe and that the experience will be one of happiness and joy. If for any reason you don't like what you are feeling, simply open your eyes, for you are totally in control. Part way through this first spell, you may want to open your eyes anyway, just to reassure yourself that you are running this show. Don't worry, it will still work.

1. Sit in a comfortable chair in a secure and quiet place. Take a deep breath through your nose, hold it for the count of three and exhale through your lips. Relax, letting your whole body slump. Repeat three times.

2. Now, with your sharp imagination, draw a band of golden light around you and the chair. It hovers a few inches above the floor. Great! Imagine that your entire body and head are enveloped in a comforting, misty white shawl of shimmering light. It is glittering with tiny, sparkling diamonds. It is see-through and airy enough to breathe through comfortably. You feel extremely safe and secure inside this cocoon of cosmic light. See it surrounding you from below your feet to about 10 or 12 inches above your head. Good! You are totally protected and your vibrations are raised to a higher level.

3. Raise your left arm and make a fist with your thumb tucked inside.

I'll tell you more about this magickal gesture, later. Ask the Great Mother and all your spirit guides to be with you. Say out loud:

> **May my guardian spirits and the spirits of the four sacred compass points support me.**

> **Welcome fine spirits of the North, East, South, and West.**

4. Then whisper:

> **Great Mother Mine, please bring forward my ancient Clan Mothers.**

> **I greet them with love and request that they may serve as my divine teachers.**

5. Lower your arm but hold the fist. Relax. Now feel a whoosh of warm energy swirling about you. It is good and kind and loving. It feels terrific. Then imagine that a bright golden energy from your fist is moving up your arm and through your body, spreading a comforting feeling of relief and peace. Take a deep breath and exhale, making a strong *"Ahhh..."* sound.

6. Say:

> **Hello, my Elders and Wisewomen. Welcome.**

> **Be with me to guide and support me as I walk the Path of the Goddess.**

> **Fill me with happiness. Breathe me joy. Breathe me light.**

7. Now completely relax and experience a sensation of pure joy. Recall your feelings at a time when you were absolutely the happiest. Let a surge of warmth

race through your body from your head to the tips of your toes. It almost makes you giddy. The top of your head feels prickly. Stay in that place of well-being for a moment.

Then say:

> **Thank you, Clan Mothers.**
>
> **May I always live with your constant love and approval.**
>
> **Thanks be to the Spirits of the North, the East, the South, the West.**
>
> **You are released.**
>
> **Thanks be to the Great Mother for this experience of joyful Mother-love.**
>
> **Blessed be.**

You did it. You conjured joy and met the Clanswomen who love you. Open your eyes wide, you amazing maiden, you accomplished Apprentice. You just created some beautiful magick. And may that fine feeling of Clan Mother love stay with you, now and always.

chapter 3

Declaring Your Rightful Place in the Clan

I believe you are now ready to take your first spiritual step by swearing a private declaration of intent. *"I am?"* you ask. Of course you are. You have nothing to lose—quite the opposite, for there is much to gain. It's time to lay claim to your rich and mystical legacy, to proudly take your rightful place at the table of the worldwide sisterhood of women who follow the Goddess Path.

How do you do that? Simply by declaring yourself to the Forces of Good with a short incantation that you can do alone or with friends. Giving voice to your "Great Declaration" is the first step on the Path to knowing the magickal wonders of embracing the Goddess and enjoying that warm and supportive feeling of truly belonging.

But first, a very important check stop—be entirely sure that your heart is full of the best intent. The purest intent. This means that you will use your spiritual knowledge and your Maiden Magick only for the good and will harm absolutely no one knowingly. Ever. This is a basic code of the women's spiritual movement, passed down through antiquity by our Clan Mothers. Exercising your faith in the Goddess is powerful magick. Promising never to use it to harm anyone is a necessary and kindly act. No negotiating on this—harm no one.

Agreed? Say so out loud. Great. Now, let's jump right in. Oh, but since you won't learn the Art of Protection until a later chapter, I'll do that job for you right now. There. You are completely surrounded with strong protection. Enjoy your ritual.

Raise your left hand and make a tight fist (thumb inside your fingers). Hold it straight-armed out before you, level with your face. With the book in your right hand, look skyward and say the words of your Great Declaration three times with heartfelt conviction, getting stronger and louder each time you repeat them. By the third repetition you should be shouting out with great Goddess gusto. Why? Because the Goddess wants you to be strong and confident. She wants you to stand up and be counted in this world. So declare yourself with strong intent and a good fire in your belly.

Why three times, you wonder? Well, three is a sacred number that goes all the way back to the mystical Druid teachers. The Clan Mothers taught me to think of it this way: You read the first declaration aloud *so that your mind may understand it*. Then lower your arm, take a deep breath, exhale, and raise your power fist again. Make your declaration the second time (louder and with more feeling) *so that your heart may feel it*. Once again, drop your arm, take another deep-into-your-lungs breath, exhale, raise that strong, capable arm with Clan-like determination, squeeze your fist and hear your voice shout your declaration to the skies above *so that your soul may own it*.

This is the formal declaration of a novice apprentice. It is a confirmation of self and it is the first ritual spell that will transform your mind and set you firmly on the path of spiritual growth, soul expansion and elevated self-esteem. Acknowledging that the Goddess dwells within you makes you part human maiden with a great big dollop of the glorious and loving Divine living right inside. How can you go wrong? Let's do it. Lift your eyes and your voice to the heavens and say out loud:

> **Good Forces of the Universe, hear me!**
> **I am_____ (your name)_____ .**
> **I belong to the Goddess Clan.**
>
> **I am a woman, dearly loved.**
> **I am a woman, much adored.**
> **I am a woman, deeply cherished.**
> **I am a beloved maiden of the Clan.**
>
> **Embraced by the sisterhood of women,**
> **Good Forces, I declare**
> **I am...and have always been**
> **A rightful and gifted**
> **Daughter of the Goddess.**
>
> **Great Mother Mine,**
> **Treasure me—as I do Thee.**
> **Blessed by Three.**
> **Blessed Be.**

How do you feel? Good? Strong? Vibrating a bit from the mystical power created by your ritual? You bet you are! And it's true. You are all those things you shouted out—loved, adored, and cherished—and you truly belong to the timeless Clan devoted to the Goddess. The spirits of your ancestors, your Clan Mothers, are with you still. Can you feel their presence?

They are, this very minute, rejoicing at the strength of your good intent, of your fabulous declaration. Believe it. You carry the powerful remnants of their life experiences stamped in your inherited genes; their ancient and enduring beliefs are embedded in your spiritual DNA.

The words "Blessed by Three" refer to the three faces or life phases of the Goddess—the same phases we women pass through here on Abred. First is the young maiden, the Apprentice, or what we now call the teen Goddess (you); then the mother with a child that may represent the birthing of a baby or a career or a creative pursuit; and, finally, the old crone—made wise and resilient from life's hard knocks (me). You are part of this natural woman's cycle, this all-encompassing and loving sorority of women who came before you and who now welcome you warmly into the fold.

You are a spiritual Apprentice on a mission of discovery and joy.

chapter 4

Reading Animal Omens That Cross Your Path

The Celtic Clan Mothers taught young lasses to sharpen their animal senses—to be quick-witted as little rabbits—in order to survive the wild outside world. It isn't living and surviving in the deep, tangled forest that you worry about anymore, today it's the streets, alleys, and mall parking lots. Being street-smart is still a matter of survival and the need to be aware at all times is very real.

The Clan Mothers would tell you to give yourself a hard shake and get out of the foggy-headed zone you often walk around in. They'd say: "'Keen-up' and pay attention to everything." Become a spy, a tracker, a warrior. It is a matter of staying safe, for sure, but it is more than that. They want you to be sharp and vigilant in recognizing the signs sent to you from the spirit side of the world. There are signs and portents of change to be read in the strange things that may happen in the course of your day. Signs from the spirit world meant just for you.

Because the Celts believed that every living thing had a soul and a spirit, they put great stock in any sign or message delivered to you by spirits from the other side. This often took the form of an animal or bird, something as insignificant as a tiny sparrow, hopping about in a tree. It's true. Bestowing even little creatures with the distinction of having a soul, of being connected to the spirits of the Otherworld, naturally elevated them in importance. And if you've ever had a favorite and beloved pet in your life, you know the Clan Mothers were right—animals do have souls.

So you spot a little bird, so what? Well, a messenger won't be just any ordinary old sparrow—oh, no—it will be a strange-acting little creature, maybe even part comedian. Your bird messenger will be slightly separate and apart from the other birds, and it will be working hard to catch your attention. It may act a bit goofy, hopping closer and closer to you, limb-to-limb, instead of flying away like a normal bird. That's your first cosmic clue.

Or your sign from the Otherworld might be delivered by an ordinary alley cat that you pass by on the sidewalk. He catches your eye, then lazily follows you part way to school. Does that ever happen? He stops when you stop, sits, then gets up and follows again as soon as you turn to walk away. Such behavior, aimed at you, is another clue. Instead of shrugging it off, pay close attention. The cat knows.

Chances are, something odd (similar to that) has happened to you at some point in time. You knew something weird was up—didn't you?—but you just didn't have the tools to understand what it all meant. Well, my clever Apprentice, you were intuitive enough at the time to know that something definitely supernatural was happening on a small scale.

You may wonder,

> *C.C., are these animal omens some kind of sign from the faeries, or the little people, or are they from the spirits, like my ancestors in the Otherworld?*

I answer: Yes! to all of the above. Any of those possibilities could be true. You've experienced an omen sent to you from the Otherworld that is to be interpreted and understood for a reason. It is a message from the cosmos and may come from many possible spiritual sources. But once you sense the presence of spiritual signs, what do you do then?

How to figure out what the omens mean

The Clans Mothers say that once you become aware of an animal messenger, you need to acknowledge that you understand it is trying to reach you. Duh...We can be such boneheads sometimes, yet the little creatures work so hard to grab our attention. So brain-up. Once the signal goes off in your mind that this may be a messenger—react.

The first step is to smile and whisper: "Thanks be" to the bold little bird, or the grinning cat, or whatever it is. Acknowledge that you're on their wavelength, and that you know they're bringing a sign or message for you.

This is most important: Once you've clued-in and said so, pay close attention to your first thoughts. When you become aware of the messengers in your daily life, it is best to absolutely trust your initial instinct. This may take a bit of practice, but you have to relax and trust your thoughts. When a bird or animal makes eye contact, or somehow works to make you aware of its presence, take note of the very first thing that springs into your mind—without really thinking about it or working at it. Why? Because that first thought is most likely what the Goddess spirits are trying to tell you. You may think of the name of a loved one here, or in the Otherworld, so say hello to that person or spirit.

Or the little messenger is there to warn you, to keep you on your toes. If you feel that, take heed immediately, sharpen your mind and "keen-up" your survival senses.

Sometimes a messenger may appear in order to encourage you, to comfort you, or simply to remind you that kindly spirits are with you, to love and support you, and offer a bit of reassurance. Now that's a sweet message, indeed.

Recognizing omens, portents, and signs from Nature are all part of developing your natural Maiden Magick. It is the Goddess Way that you will soon come to understand intuitively. It's delightful green magick, and it will soon be part of your kit bag of Maiden Magick tricks.

⧼⧽

A quick way to interpret signs and omens is to check out the following Celtic charts of birds and animals. If you are very fortunate, use the third chart to interpret what a faerie visit means. Although it is serious magick, it's also great fun.

I've also left space for a journal so you can record what you saw, what you thought it meant at the time, and anything that happens later that relates to the sighting. It may be something small and seemingly insignificant, because you are just beginning to read omens and the good spirits will likely give you easy messages to interpret at first for encouragement. Remember to practice. Practice makes your Maiden Magick feel familiar and comfortable and it improves your skills. The Goddess is delighted you are beginning to develop your intuitive self, your natural magickal talents. Good for you.

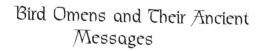

Bird Omens and Their Ancient Messages

All Birds
Because of their ability to fly, birds were considered to be human spirits, temporarily released from the prison of their bodies, who carried greetings from those you love in the Otherworld. Celts studied birds carefully and used their movements and calls to predict the future. Always say a warm "hello" to any bird that catches your eye.

Songbirds
Songbirds are some of the happiest of omens. They were considered truly supernatural creatures with the ability to heal hearts, ease physical ills, and cure all kinds of spiritual anguish. Lucky you to hear a songbird! It is always a fortunate omen as you will know by the lift you feel just hearing its song.

Wrens
Welsh Celts considered wrens to be related to the sun spirit, Bel, and used them in Springtime rituals. If you spot a wren flying overhead, it can be interpreted as a fast-coming change in your life—like Winter bursting into Spring. Consider letting go of a worrisome situation that weighs on your spirit and consciously move to a quieter, calmer place in your soul.

Crows and Ravens
Considered by some to be harbingers of darkness, doom, and death, these birds (crows are the smaller guys) got their bad

reputation because they were scavengers who haunted the battlefields. As scavengers or "cleaners" of the Earth, they were also present in large flocks when the people died of the Black Plague. You can imagine that sight alone was enough to give them a bad image.

On the flip side, crows and ravens are also considered by many (including me) to be positive portents, because they were the most common companions to the Celtic goddesses. The Celts in Scotland called wisdom and the ability to see the future "Raven-knowledge." Crows and ravens are highly intelligent and they are excellent survivors. I always greet them happily as messengers who bring a fond hello from female ancestors, or as a sign that a healing of some kind is most likely in your future. On the fun side, it was believed that crows let the faeries climb onto their backs for rides to faraway destinations—akin to an airborne taxi or a 727 jet. Can't you just picture it?

Be of good cheer if you meet one and it looks you in the eye. Don't cringe. Crows and ravens are not necessarily negative, simply trust your instincts and listen to that first clear voice in your head when you see or hear one cawing. All things considered, I'd take the presence of Grandmother Crow in my day as a positive, though noisy, omen.

Swans

Swans are the real celebrities in many Celtic legends of transformation and rescue. This is a very good sign. Interpret a Swan's appearance in your life as most positive. It symbolized purity of heart, divine and sexual love, and lifelong fidelity. Wow! I'd gladly take any one of those blessings.

Ducks

Ducks were a companion of the Celtic Goddess Sequana—She even had one carved on the prow of her boat! Ducks are healing spirits and, as the harbingers of Spring, they bring to you a message of rebirth and foretell of easier times ahead.

The Crane

This is a good sign—or a not-so-good sign. You decide. On the positive side, the crane was the deliverer of newborn souls (the baby stork) and it foretold of all the happiness that a birth event brings. On the negative side, it could mean darkness associated with unpleasant, nagging females.

Maybe it's time to quit that awful part-time job where the nasty female boss drives you half-crazy. Then again, maybe it's a message that encourages you to begin anew by taking up a creative project as a form of rebirth. Listen carefully to what the crane says to you.

Check Out What These Animal Omens Mean

Dog: Protection, hearth, home, fidelity, faithfulness, family.

Small Dog: Soothing comfort and relief. Used as an ancient "hot water bottle," a small dog cuddled up on your lap would help relieve menstrual cramps (and it made the puppy feel very loved).

Snake: Good fortune (despite what some people think). Healing and regeneration. Also, because it sheds its skin, it means time to consider a major adjustment in your lifestyle. Serpents are sacred to the Goddess.

Cat: Clever. Self-sufficient. A cat signals a time to be clever and to take the lead to disassociate yourself from some upsetting situation.

Rabbit: A blessing/A blessed warning. The Hare was sacred to the Goddess Brigit and a lucky omen—hence the rabbit's foot charm. But if the rabbit runs right across your path, it's not so good. It is a warning. Be really careful, keen-up your senses that day, and listen to your heart. You'll learn something and all will be fine.

Bees: The sweet conclusion to a problem. Good, unexpected news. The Druids paid reverence to the bee and the Celts drank barrels of delicious alcoholic honey mead, also in reverence? Umm...I don't think so. Bees are magickal, they can give you the courage to change things.

DEER: Raw nature. Sexuality. Fertility. The deer was to the Goddess what the stag was to a king. Passion. First two parts are fun, but watch out for the "fertility" part of the omen—unless you want that result.

GOAT: Money. Prosperity. Fertilization of an idea or project. How many goats are you going to see on any given day? Not enough it seems since they are such good luck. But just in case you're in farm country, here are two more to watch out for:

COW: Abundance. Soul nourishment. Spirituality. Any cow is good, but a white cow is remarkable. It symbolized everything good on the Earth to the Goddess. Paint mine white.

PIG: Very good luck. Regeneration or a happy second chance. Celts believed pigs are from the Otherworld and signify endless renewal. It is a sign of eating your cake, but still having it. If you are in the city, you can have the same great results by cutting out the picture of a pig and tucking it in your pocket or notebook.

Wait! I Think I Saw a Faerie!

I was 5 years old when I first saw a ring of faeries dancing in the grass. Mesmerized, I watched for a long time, then ran to get my mother. When we returned there was a brown circle scorched on the grass where the little dancers had been.

"Ah," she said matter-of-factly, "there's no doubt. You definitely saw the faeries." It is a happy memory that remains as fresh and as exciting as though it happened only yesterday. I felt enchanted and blessed.

Do you think you may have seen or felt the presence of a faerie or two? It's possible. Here's what the Clan Mothers would say it means:

FAERIE: Blessed you. Did you catch the flutter of a faerie in your peripheral vision? The edge of a wing or the rustle of a silk gown? Did you hear the tinkling bell sound of their laughter? Or did you just have a "feeling" about it? You can label that delightful experience as a true Goddess blessing. Lucky you. It means you are about to have a terrific run of happy days and, best of all, the little people say you'll have a most charmed life.

Just remember to say: *Faeries, I believe in you.*
Don't trick me.

They'll respect that and you'll enjoy the gift of their kind attention.

Journaling—
Scribble Down Your Divine Thoughts

Day one:

WHAT I SAW TODAY THAT I'M SURE WAS AN OMEN:

THE THOUGHTS THAT POPPED INTO MY HEAD WHEN IT HAPPENED:

WHAT THE CELTIC CLAN MOTHERS SAID IT MIGHT MEAN:

FOLLOW-UP (WHAT HAPPENED LATER):

Another day:

WHAT I SAW TODAY THAT MAY HAVE BEEN AN OMEN:

THE THOUGHTS THAT POPPED INTO MY HEAD WHEN IT HAPPENED:

WHAT THE CELTIC CLAN MOTHERS SAID IT MIGHT MEAN:

FOLLOW-UP:

Yet another day, another omen:

WHAT I SAW TODAY THAT MAY HAVE BEEN AN OMEN:

THE THOUGHTS THAT POPPED INTO MY HEAD WHEN IT HAPPENED:

WHAT THE CELTIC CLAN MOTHERS SAID ABOUT IT:

FOLLOW-UP:

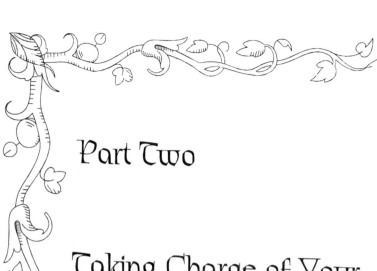

Part Two

Taking Charge of Your Spiritual Quest

chapter 5
Button Up Your Bulletproof Vest

Magickal Maidens soon discover that life is made up of ever revolving cycles or circles—everything that goes around, comes back around, as they say—and that's good news. Why? When you're feeling blue and everything seems dark and hopeless, you can count on the Celtic fact that the cycle will change and come back up again, eventually your life will always improve.

But Auntie, what if I'm feeling really up,
does that mean…?

Well, yeah, it does. It means it won't last forever. But you know that already, don't you? You've already experienced changes of all sorts in your life and fortunes. Yet by understanding that there are cycles in life, you will become more aware of your feelings and more alert to change. By knowing in your Magick Maiden heart that good times come and go, you have two great advantages: you will have the incentive to make the very most of those good times when they do appear; and you will have the good sense to anticipate and prepare for change because it is inevitable. Flexibility, my dear Apprentice, is everything.

Here is a Clan Mother fact: The act of "knowing" makes you stronger. With your women's knowledge of life's natural cycles, of knowing that even good things will change, dull down or go sour, you still win. Instead of drifting aimlessly through life, pretending the good times will last forever, you can turn your energies to the job of *appreciating* all the great things and all the happiness you are experiencing at the moment *to the very fullest*—and that's not a bad thing to do. Loving harder, laughing louder, dancing barefoot in the sunshine—you won't miss a single blissful moment in your life, will you?

Learning from nature

The Clan Mothers studied Mother Moon as she moved through her phases, from starless darkness to the silver of a full moon's light, every 28 days. As an Apprentice, you need to acknowledge the revolving presence of both the lightness and the darkness that is naturally built into your long spiritual journey. Much like the season's cycles, your life will evolve. Only by accepting the Celtic truth that there is always a "flip side" to everything, will you be ready for all the good and bad that life will shovel your way. Facing this truth of light and darkness, side by side, will allow you to be strong and to protect yourself from the hardships here on Abred, or from the wily tricksters in the spirit realm of the Otherworld.

Protecting yourself on two planes—Abred and the Otherworld

Life is full of joys...and equally fraught with dangers. Accepting this ancient truth makes practical and spiritual sense. Celtic maidens were cautioned against dangers that might be lurking in the dark forest or in the Otherworld. But today, your medieval forest is the urban street, the dark alley, or the empty parking lot, isn't it? They are totally different places—but pose similar dangers. Apprentices were taught to approach everything with a healthy dash of knowing Maiden caution and care.

On the practical side, they studied how to wield a heavy sword or a two-sided ax. After their initiation, they kept a razor-sharp dagger in their belt. What can you do today? Sign up for a good self-defense course for women to give you street-warrior skills and confidence. Get fit so you can run fast as the wind, and know it. Always use your intuitive animal instincts to sniff out danger and to avoid ever becoming prey. Take decisive action. Be an accomplished warrior Goddess every day. But in addition to these practical survival skills, the early spiritual Apprentices mastered the magickal skills of spiritual self-protection. So can you.

Women, then as now, were natural healers and nurturers, serving as the tribal herbalists, the doctors, midwives, and spiritual counselors to maidens in training like you are. Though these skilled women encountered the darker side of life in each of those professions, they chose to concentrate on the numinous light—the Goddess light—to serve them in their work. They conjured up the Forces of Good to fix people, to bring babies safely into the world, and to give wise and knowing advice to a young person experiencing pain and confusion.

These sensible women also used their spiritual skills to protect themselves and their patients from the spirit rascals and troublemakers who lurk in the shadows, or in that place of limbo found between the worlds. These lesser beings could be a pesky aggravation, or they could cause serious trouble. So all Goddess practitioners mastered the steps for casting a strong spell of protection—a wall of impenetrable light against tricks and trouble—before proceeding in their spiritual work. It was called *casting their Lorica*.

Ancient truth of the Lorica

Centuries ago, the Clan Mothers would dip into their storehouse of old legends and tales to teach you the timeless skill of women's "knowing." There are many ancient stories about the magickal suit of armor that protects the spirit and soul from intruders, or from those intent on causing harm. It was known as the Celtic breastplate of protection, or the Lorica. There are even tales of Saint Patrick making use of this ancient gear to keep harm away. I can't stress enough how important the Lorica is to your spiritual Apprenticeship. Protection must be summoned before beginning every spell or blessing, ritual or ceremony.

Your Lorica can be quickly conjured by focusing your concentration during the strong self-protection spell that I will teach you. But you must pledge to make it a second-nature and automatic ritual that you use regularly and systematically because, as a practitioner of the Forces of Good, you must be protected always.

My own Lorica story

In a particularly sad and stressful time in my life, sleep would not come and worries bombarded me. I found myself lying in bed, stiff and rigid at 3 a.m. Then the Clan Mothers spoke to me and urged me to call on the ancient Lorica of protection.

I quickly took three deep breaths and imagined my Lorica, not as hammered steel, but as a long blue cashmere robe with a big hood. I saw it wrapped around my chilled body from my toes up to and covering my head. It was soft and warm—the very protection from the unkind, cold world I needed at that moment. I breathed a sigh of relief and relaxed within its imagined comfort and protection. I slept soundly for the first time in weeks and from then on my life began to change for the better. My cycle had bottomed out and I was pushing upwards again. My Lorica of protection, my own warrior's breastplate of armor, saved me from my own dark and hopeless thoughts. It will do the same for you, Spiritual Seeker. That you can count on.

How to "Conjure-Up"

You've watched *Buffy the Vampire Slayer*, and you've read lots about magick, so you know what conjuring a spell is about—but how do you do it, exactly?

To conjure means to call upon by ritual or command as you do in a spell. That much you know. Yet the basis of a spell's success begins in your imagination. You may have noticed that I've asked you to imagine this or that. This is because everything worthwhile begins in the imagination. The very skill of creative imagination is the link between the seen and the unseen. Even the great psychiatrist and psychologist, Carl Jung (pronounced Young), paid great tribute to the powers of the active imagination. Don't sell your imagination short! Imagination is the key to living "betwixt and between."

Exercising the full scope of the imagination was easier for Celtic maidens long ago because their tradition was primarily oral, and so they'd sit around a crackling fire and listen to great colorful tales of suspense and danger involving beautiful maidens, like you, and equally dashing lads with piercing blue eyes and incredible strength. They would be required to fill in all the vivid details with their imagination, up to and including the fetid stench and searing heat of the pursuing dragon's breath. Run, run, run.

That's what happens when you live in a world where words conjure images (there's that word again). And words still do call up images. Our imaginations are just a little rusty because we are bombarded by so many "real" images every day (in print and on screen), that don't require much participation from our imagination. I'd wager that you do have a keen imagination, but in today's world people usually sit and watch more than they create. So, when the time comes to cast a Spell of Protection, you'll have to give your sleepy imagination a good swift kick and say: "Hey, Rip Van Winkle...wake up!"

When and Where to Use Your Lorica

When do you use this self-protection spell? Almost every day. The Lorica is multipurpose and will serve to protect you, and those you love and care about. Here's when and where to use it:

1. To protect your spells.

Conjure up your Lorica before each and every spell you cast. It is absolutely essential. Don't let me down on this one. A quick Lorica is your guarantee of casting uninterrupted and energizing magickal powers; it is your assurance that all the intent you put into your blessings, healings, or spells of good fortune will work its magick. Like American Express credit cards: Don't cast a spell without it.

2. To protect friends and family.

Conjure up your Lorica to cast a impenetrable Circle of Protection around someone you love even if you aren't doing a spell. Imagine the possibilities and the power the Lorica gives you. You can cast a light around an airplane they are about to take, or a hospital they need to enter, or even around a situation at school or work that is vexing them, making them stressed or unhappy. You simply cast it, see it protecting them, bringing positive results, then forget it. Relax and stop worrying because they will be surrounded by the protective love of the Goddess and all the Forces of Good.

3. To protect yourself.

Conjure up your protective Lorica whenever you feel fear, or feel threatened, or you are overcome by stress or illness. Even at night, when you can't sleep and your head fills with worries and nightmarish thoughts, take a moment to cast your Lorica. It is your psychic shield. Your stone wall to keep harmful, debilitating thoughts out. It is your comfort, your cosmic protector. Use it often.

Casting the Lorica—Your Own Spell of Protection

This is an important spell that requires some preparation in advance, so set a few minutes aside the first time you conjure the Spell of Protection.

Oh, bummer...you wanted to get right to it, I suppose. Well, here's the cool part—at the end of this spell, you will lock in its protective magick using a physical trigger, so that whenever—and wherever—you feel the need of protection, you got it. It's yours forever, in an instant, a nanosecond or, as the Clan Mothers would say, "In a heartbeat." It is worth a little work.

Preparation in advance of casting your spell

Sit somewhere quiet where you won't be bothered by anyone. Imagine your Lorica. What will your cosmic protective armor look like? Take your time. It's your creation and there are no rules. See it in your mind in great detail, right down to the feel and texture of its surface, to its weight as you heft it up to put it on. Design it any way you want. As you do, believe without a doubt, that your Lorica will be impenetrable. It will keep you safe. Remember: As you believe, so shall it be.

Strap on your protective armor

Take three deep breaths and relax after each. Let your shoulders drop and your body slump slightly. Imagine that each breath brings in pure Goddess power and expels all doubt. Know that the loving spirits are pulling for you. Everyone loves you. The Goddess stands by you. No worries.

Study your Lorica of Protection. See it clearly. Take a moment to examine it. Turn it this way and that in your mind. Be aware of its appearance: its size, texture, and color. Feel its weight. It is a perfect Lorica for you, isn't it? You will feel as protected as an ancient warrior when you wear it, believe me. Now, as with all good magick, state your intentions. Speak directly to your Lorica in a tone that is kindly—but firm:

"Lorica Mine, serve me well." Excellent.

Now it's time to try it on, time to take full possession of your Lorica. If it is metal, chain mail, or a hard, leathery armor of some kind, picture yourself strapping it on and buckling the straps in place. Adjust it until it sits comfortably on your shoulders like a second skin. Say, you are looking mighty fine. Invincible—like the warrior goddess you are.

If your Lorica is crafted from a fabric, or made of warm soft wool (like my own Lorica), or woven together from nature's grasses and sticks and leaves, you may want to pick it up, sniff its natural fragrance and wrap yourself in its sweet comfort. Don't be shy—claim it—it is yours, and yours alone. Hey, consider this a cosmic fashion show of sorts. You are on the runway, the cameras are rolling, strobe lights flashing, and there's that buzz in the crowd that spells excitement and anticipation because you are…absolutely fabulous!

Now address the Goddess with heartfelt conviction in your voice:

> **Great Mother Mine, come nigh to me**
> **as I cast my everlasting Lorica,**
> **my protection from unseen forces and cosmic**
> **tricksters.**
> **Bless my Lorica spell.**
>
> **Make it steely strong.**
> **Hear me as I dedicate my life,**
> **my work, and my magick**
> **to the Forces of Good.**
>
> **Blessed be.**

Terrific. She'll be pleased. And you feel rather good too, don't you?

Now the next step…in your mind, wrap a white cloud-like mist of shimmering light all around the image of you in your Lorica. See the light of protection sparkling all about you. What a wonderful feeling! Do you feel it? Take your time until you feel the strength of that reassuring, protective light. Stand tall in the comfort of its warm embrace.

A magickal trigger to conjure your Lorica

Wow, that took quite a while, didn't it? You can't go through all that every time you need protection, can you? There's just not enough time. What you need is a physical trigger to bring that magickal power back in a flash.

Simply do this: Take the index and the middle finger of your right hand and raise them to touch your third eye—that Magickal place of knowing and seeing that is between your eyebrows, just above your nose. Tap this spot three times so you are physically aware of the touch and say out loud:

> **Great Mother Mine.**
> **By the magick of my Lorica, forever anon,**
> **Protect me.**

There. You and those you love will be protected. You have conjured a personal and powerful magick spell, and created a physical trigger to summon your protection on demand. What amazing Goddess Magick!

Calling up your Lorica instantly

In the future, whenever you cast a spell, create a ritual, take part in a ceremony, or weave a blessing—always protect yourself first. Just touch those two fingers to your third eye to call up your protection, instantly. You may ask the Great Mother for protection at the same time, but words are not really needed. The trigger of touch and memory is sufficient.

No time to touch your forehead? No problem. Just imagine the feel of your fingertips on your forehead and cast the protective light around yourself and those you wish to protect. Even that will work. Don't forget, it's magick. Maiden Magick at its very best in action.

BLESSED BE, YOU CLEVER GIRL.

chapter 6

Pamper Your Soul Through Self Blessing

Check out this ancient code for walking the Goddess Path. It is deceptively simple, yet it is often ignored by most young Spiritual Seekers. Here's your Goddess truth:

BE TRUE TO THYSELF.

Yeah, C.C. I've heard that before. It's Shakespeare or something....

Almost right. He wrote, "To thine own self be true." Same thinking. But then, Shakespeare got plenty of material and inspiration from the Celts' doctrines and rituals. For you, as an Apprentice, it is a foundation lesson for walking the Goddess Path correctly. This ancient Celtic code for living has been found carved into the mega-stones in burial mounds that are thousands of years old. This Goddess lesson was literally carved-in-stone to remind you to honor yourself. Live life your way. Do what rings true to you. It speaks to the absolute importance of considering what is right for *you* and the lifelong importance of living your own truth. Period.

Think about your life so far. Are you racing about, marching to the tune of others? Have you sat down and considered what you want, what you need, what is important to you? Well, isn't it time you got to know yourself better? Gave yourself more credit? Counted your many gifts and your talents? Honored the incredible beauty of who you are? It is a key for living successfully that comes down to you from antiquity.

The Clan Mothers, the Celtic Aunties, taught their apprentices to accept this law: You are the center of your own life, you create all that happens, you run the ship. If that is so, then you need to be absolutely sure that your life truly and honestly reflects your heart and soul's desire. Because no matter what happens, good or bad, you wear it.

Now, concentrating on yourself seems to contradict everything that older adults are telling you today, doesn't it? They harp on you about thinking more about others, not yourself. In fact, caring about yourself, taking time to develop your intellectual and spiritual self, and fully realizing the extent of your personal potential, are self-knowledge actions that go hand-in-hand with the ability to truly care about others. Those two acts (self-development and genuine caring) are complementary. When you take "care" with yourself, you grow stronger, more resilient, and frankly—you have more to give back, with less effort.

Being "true to thyself" doesn't mean being narrowly self-involved and not giving a flying hoot about other people. Not at all. It means that you are aware of the importance of becoming all you have the potential to be on Abred, and your full potential includes serving up a heaping plate of generosity and loving kindness to others along your journey. It's an integral part of the whole soul package. The bigger your soul grows, the more readily and naturally you will share with others.

It is a bit mind-boggling, but it makes real goddess sense. It is time to open your spiritual eyes wide to the truth of who you are. Begin to see and experience the amazing wonder of you. Acknowledge the complexity of your intellectual self, your creative self, your emotional, spiritual, and fun-loving self. Decide that the most important project right now is your development, and realize your full potential as a strong, courageous, and admirable woman of intuitive magick, talent, and sensitivity. Don't turn your back on the needs of others, but do consider your own.

It won't be easy because such a code flies in the face of most social conventions. No one said that walking the Goddess Path would be easy. Strangely enough, giving yourself the boost of confidence you need to succeed can be one of the hardest parts. But as a spiritual apprentice walking the Goddess Path, you must concentrate on your spiritual and personal expansion and development. By learning self-reliance and self-responsibility, you will enjoy the natural side effects of a rise in your self-worth and the kick of becoming truly comfortable within yourself.

And there is another groovy bonus: Once you believe in yourself, are true to your nature, and become comfortable in your own sneakers, you will begin to attract kindred spirits into your life. Giving and loving and caring just grow easier, more natural. Once you are clear about who you are, and what you can be with sustained effort, then like-minded friends and even lovers of equal personal strength are easily attracted to you. Like draws like. If you want more in friends or an awesome lover, don't run about helter-skelter or sit home brooding. Get to work recreating yourself as an even better person. The rest will flow into place as naturally as a stream slipping over the smooth stones.

Promise?

Well, my dear apprentice, Auntie C.C., along with the help of those wily crones, the Clan Mothers, not only promises that your life will improve when you learn to walk the Goddess Path, we absolutely guarantee it.

As the Clan Mothers taught, it all begins and ends with you. The harder you work to grow and expand your mind, heart, and soul, the better your life will be. That doesn't mean you won't have your challenges—oh, no. Challenges are how we learn. What *does* change is your attitude. When life's hard lessons knock you over, your strength of character will pick you up, brush you off, and get you safely back on your Goddess Path.

Now, let's begin with a Self-Blessing. Imagine! Blessing yourself! Brash isn't it? But don't be shy. Ask yourself this: "Who best deserves the blessing of the Goddess who dwells within my heart and soul?" Correct and only answer? No one but *you*! You deserve the best.

Start by making the following Self-Blessing part of your everyday life. Say it often, until you have not only memorized it, but really believe it. The Goddess loves you dearly. Believe it. It's a woman's shining truth.

Self-Blessing

Commit this little invocation to memory. Carry a copy around with you and read it over and over until it is part of you. Bringing forth goodness and light is the basis of all the magick you weave, and this feel-good spell is created especially for you. Keep in mind, my apprentice, that if the Great Mother loves you so much, and believes you are so terrific, then who are you to argue? It has to be true. You truly have great worth.

Great Mother Mine, now I can see
You crafted a world full of beauty
And with that same magick
You then crafted...*me*.

Fill me, too, with grace and wit.
Add songs, dance, and merriment.

Fill me with vision and insight high.
Add belief in myself so my soul can fly.

Fill me with talent and a mind so bright.
Add kindness, goodness, and a heart of light.

Great Mother Mine, now I can see
You crafted a world full of beauty.
And with that same magick,
You then crafted...*me*.

As I love You, so I love me.
Blessed by Three,
Blessed Be.

chapter 7

Step Forward With Genuine Confidence

Wouldn't it be great to walk to the front of a crowded classroom and take a seat feeling good about yourself, maybe even smiling? Or later in your life Path, when it comes time to choose a job or profession for yourself, wouldn't it be super to reach for the top? To really go for it, like you can be anything you want? Maybe you secretly dream of being a doctor or lawyer, or a successful musician, or maybe you want to open your own makeup studio, or art studio, or anything else that seems far beyond your reach right now. It all comes down to building a sense of self as strong as a fortress inside you, and beginning to appreciate your unique and Goddess-given abilities.

You can develop the self-esteem you need not to feel intimidated at school (if you do sometimes), or to go out and make new friends, or even to plan and design a life for yourself that will be fulfilling. As your spiritual guide and Celtic Auntie, let me say right now—you can be anything you put your heart to. That's right, anything. You can achieve anything you desire, you can feel good about yourself, and you can look forward to reaching a comfortable state of contentment and joy. How? With faith in the Goddess. Believing in yourself takes a combination of *two* important elements. You must start by taking these steps:

1. Develop an abiding spiritual belief in the divine aspects of your soul where the Goddess dwells, for to believe in the Goddess within is to believe in yourself.

2. Develop personal initiative and the roll-up-your-sleeves kind of attitude that make good things naturally happen for you.

The confidence of knowing you are part divine

For apprentices in ancient times, the foundation of strong self-esteem was based on the belief that the Goddess lives within every woman's soul. How can you feel badly about yourself when you are part of the Goddess force, when you are part divine? If you honor Her, you honor yourself. It was that simple and that clear.

Today, it is the same for you. To accept and believe in the incredible powers of the feminine deity in all creation means you are an integral part of that natural magick. This knowledge allows you to see yourself in a better light, in a kinder light. Love Her. Love yourself. As you absorb this knowledge, you will grow to accept all that you are, and to appreciate all that you have the potential to become. You will begin to glow with confidence and kindness.

Get closer to your feminine divine by practicing helpful spells, healings, and blessings. Write chants and learn to do affirmations. Fill your life with laughter and kindred friends. Learn the history of the Goddess faith, always help others, and begin to reach out and practice the comforting sisterhood of women helping women. Open yourself to the joy around you. Newfound self-esteem and confidence will be its natural companion.

The confidence that comes with positive action

Now, what do you do with this empowering information that comes from walking the Goddess Path? You act on it; you make things happen. You see life and wonderful possibilities opening up for you. You believe that you can make your dreams come true, that you can create the kind of life you want to live. You begin to take responsibility for yourself, for your actions, and for your responses to the challenges encountered along your spiritual journey.

Start by getting in the habit of finding positive solutions to problems in your life. Don't be torpedoed by your lack of money, or your family situation, or even by past pain. Refuse to be a victim. You are a strong and confident emissary of the Goddess, not a pitiful victim. Put that behind you and live life anew. Proceed along your life Path as though there are no obstacles, no real barriers to your success. You'll be surprised to find that what you thought were barriers, or troublesome people, or insurmountable obstacles no longer stop you. At least not for long...

Belief in yourself is part of the Old Way, and part of walking the Goddess Path. You are a beautiful spirit. She knows it. And soon, so will you.

How to Design Your Own Magickal Chants

There are a number of different kinds of spells. The invocation and incantation are the most common. An invocation spell calls on a higher power to "invoke" help; an incantation is used to get the spell-maker into a proper frame of mind to create magick. Frequent repetition allows the intuitive to shine through, and a lilting or chanting rhythm serves to raise the intent of the spell, clearly separating it from ordinary, everyday speech and making it sacred. Effective chants make good use of rhyme, rhythm, and repetition, much the way a popular rock song does. "Catchy tunes" that you just can't get out of your head often change your mood and outlook, don't they? They are a tried-and-true version of old Celtic chants that the Bards or High Priestesses sang.

Let's start with a chant of self-blessing because you need to get yourself as strong and clear as possible before you go on to casting spells to help others. Here's a great example by Valerie Worth, an excellent poet and spell-maker. This is only a part of her spell, *For Success on an Important Occasion*. Thanks be to the creative gifts of Valerie Worth. In this spell, she suggests you lie in a herbal bath (our Celtic Cauldron) and repeat three times.

> **I shall bathe**
> **And I shall be**
> **As green and strong,**
> **Good herbs, as thee;**

Draw me favor,
Draw me fame.
Draw bright honor
To my name.

———Valerie Worth, *The Crone's Book of Words*

See how bold you need to be? Self-blessings are not a time to be timid or shy. As an apprentice of the Goddess Way, you need to reach right out there into the cosmos and draw down good energy and encouragement to your soul. The Goddess blesses such forthright action.

The previous spell is an invocation and a chant. Valerie calls on the herbs—gifts from the Goddess—as a higher source of power, and then adds the magick of repetition and rhyme. The second and fourth lines of each stanza rhyme, and the second stanza is pure Celtic chant—the repetition of the strong action word "draw" makes it clear what the spell-maker wants to accomplish. She calls for the blessings of *favor, fame,* and *honor.* Wow! No shrinking violet here! Now, the rhyming is lovely to my Celtic ear, but it's not always necessary for an effective chant, so don't get hung up on that when you write yours.

I suggest that you go to the library or bookstore and read all the chants and blessings and affirmations you can find, so that your ear becomes accustomed to the cadence, the lilt. I highly recommend a recent book of spells and blessings by Sirona Knight called *Goddess Bless!* (Red Wheel/Weiser). It is a great reference book for you to have and it will serve as a helpmeet for your own writings. It is also so uplifting, you'll enjoy reading it daily.

Now, for your first chant. I'll get you started on the first and third line, then you fill in the blanks. Or if you prefer, take over and rewrite the whole thing.

First, think about what you want to draw to you in a higher sense—such as vision, tolerance, wisdom, or even more crazy fun which is highly regarded by the Celts (and me). Don't include material possessions, or a particular person's name, in your spells for that is a bidding, or binding, spell and it must be approached with caution and higher training. Stick to your own needs right now. And you know exactly what you need so work it into a powerful chant to make it happen. After it's finished, memorize it and repeat it on the way to school, or anytime you are alone. The more often you speak it out to the universe, the more the positive energy flows to you.

Ready to jump in? Sure you are. You are highly creative and you'll do well. Get your pen. Here's the title and some possible lines for you to play with—or discard—as you so choose:

The Goddess and I Rule

Together we love the world we see

Write the next line:

_____

Now my turn:

And alone, She says, I'll never be.

Go ahead, write the next:

_____

Good start. Tinker with it, change it until you love it and it speaks to you. Now, here's an example of the chant stanza to follow. I've used an action verb at the beginning of each line that invokes the image of the Goddess breathing gifts directly into your soul, into your life. Choose your gifts carefully, then say it with authority, for you are in control.

Breathe me _____

Breathe me _____

Breathe me _____

Beneath this day's fair sun.

Once you are finished writing your self-blessing chant, put it away for a half hour or more. Why? Because you don't want the early changes or false starts that may still be in your mind to get jumbled-up with your final chant, or final request. With spells of magick, you must guard against confusion in the message or any accidental self-cancellations of intent. So allow a little time for the writing and rewriting energy to sort itself out and clarify.

When you reread your chant, be sure it clearly states what you desire. And when you do repeat it—and do that at least three times in a row—say it in a tone of voice that is different from your normal speaking voice. Play with the sounds until you find your own spell-voice. Then chant it aloud with Goddess-conviction. You have a birthright to do so.

Well, my accomplished apprentice, may the power of your verbal magick honor the Goddess, may it bring you many blessings, and may it keep you skipping merrily down this women's Path of spiritual enlightenment. Blessed be.

Journaling—
Scribble Your Chant Creation into Being

Before you compose your chant, make these notes:

What blessings would you like the Goddess to give to you? Take the higher road.

1. _____

2. _____

3. _____

Some action verbs to use in the chant: (for example: to draw, to breathe)

_____, _____, or _____

My own self-blessing chant
Ready to write? Fire away.

chapter 8

Become the Skipper of Your Own Yacht

Now that your personal confidence is all fluffed up and you've begun to explore the depth of your spiritual awareness, it's time to take control of your life. Time to name yourself Skipper of your own beautiful yacht, sailing the seven seas of Abred.

In deciding to walk the Goddess Path, you have sent out a strong signal that you are more than willing to become responsible for your sweet soul. As a teen, the Clan Mothers encourage you to rewrite and improve your role in your family, spiff-up your image, and see yourself as a treasured and serious apprentice of the Goddess Path. They counsel you to grab hold of your everyday life; to develop your half-forgotten, fledgling talents; and to chart your course through the tangled gardens of Abred. They know the Goddess within wants you to be your very best, but most of all She wants you to walk in the light— that positive state of being from whence all good things flow.

I know a Northern Cree teacher, a very talented and compassionate woman, who works with young people your age. I am always amazed at how similar the teachings of many Aboriginal nations are to the tribal teachings of the Celtic Elders. She has a catchy phrase that both empowers her students and reminds them to take responsibility for themselves. She tells them that excuses have to be put aside. Starting right now, you are no longer a dependent child—you are 100 percent responsible for your life. She tells them this and it should become your mantra:*"If it is to be, it is up to me."*

As your Celtic Auntie, I echo her code for teens. Taking control of your life is an empowering and uplifting experience. By crafting an earth plane life that is true to yourself and your desires, you will begin to grow and to enjoy real freedom, both spiritually and in your everyday comings and goings.

If life has been difficult for you, and it often is for young people, then maybe it's time for an attitude realignment. Maybe you need to stop blaming others, or certain situations, for holding you back and making you feel childlike and powerless. As I said when we first met at the beginning of this book, you are now "of age" according to the traditions of the Celtic clans.

In the past, you may have fallen into the trap of blaming your unhappiness in life on others, or on some perceived bad deal. And that may be valid. You may be a victim of circumstances. But guess what? Not anymore. It is now time, as a follower of the Goddess, to leave all your excuses behind, whatever they are. It is time for you to take up the threads of your life and, with great care, to begin to weave them into a strong and sturdy rope that will serve you well in any eventuality.

Or perhaps, you have had a rather easy life, all things considered. Is that the case? If so, you may be on automatic pilot, simply cruising along on the security of childhood where everything was—and maybe still is—done for you. Everything is taken care of by some adult. But, as in all things, you know there is a "flip side" to that luxury of being cared for all the time, isn't there? For one, you probably don't have much to say about the direction or the responsibilities in your life. That frustration may be causing you to be grouchy, angry, and full of negative emotions, perhaps even confusion. Lack of control always does that to people and animals. All living things must be able to skipper their own boat, to have some sense of control.

But here's the catch—you can't take control unless you show, with consistency, that you are responsible; that others can count on you; and that you deserve respect. Begin, my Apprentice, by becoming self-reliant. Take charge in matters related to your own care. How so? If you don't already, begin to cook for yourself (and sometimes others). Do your own laundry; meet expectations at school cheerfully, for education is essential to success in your life Path; start making your own arrangements; and follow through on everything you do. If you can do it yourself, do. It is worth the effort.

Cast off the lethargy. Act as a young warrior Goddess preparing for the battle ahead in a world where you will have to do everything for yourself. No more leaning on others. No more being waited on. Shun the spoiling. Accept no molly-coddling. All these dependencies exact the price of your real sense of freedom and well-being. There is no sense of pride in having things done for you.

Pledge to yourself that you will take action: solid, strong, and beautiful Goddess apprentice action. You can do it all yourself; you can be responsible for yourself. Begin now. Add another little responsibility each day, until you are waltzing through life with confidence. Amaze everyone around you and watch their attitudes toward you change—for the better. You are about to experience the high that comes from improving your status within your own clan.

SELF-RESPONSIBILITY = CONTROL IN YOUR LIFE =
FREEDOM = POSITIVE EMOTIONS = HAPPINESS

A whole bushel basket of warm and wonderfully positive experience awaits you. Congratulations, Skipper.

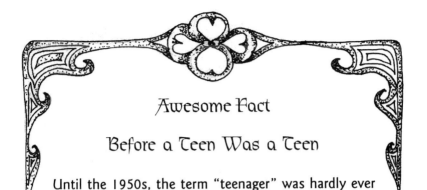

Awesome Fact

Before a Teen Was a Teen

Until the 1950s, the term "teenager" was hardly ever heard. For centuries, young women your age were considered to be in the crucial and exciting developmental stage of their life journey—with all the challenges and responsibilities that came with this wondrous time in life. Part way between the years of 12 to 19, you naturally blossomed into a full adult with all the rights and privileges that adults enjoyed. Being designated "teens" changed all that. It put your age group in a kind of long drawn-out limbo and spawned a nasty string of adjectives—lazy, troubled, rebellious, wild, spoiled—that categorized teens and diminished all expectations for those years. *Oh well, they're just teenagers, after all. Whad'ya expect?* A pretty bum rap, don't you think?

> *P.S. Check out your dictionary. Mine is a Random House/Webster's College and it gives an archaic definition for the noun "teen." Guess what? It meant "suffering; grief." Are you surprised?*

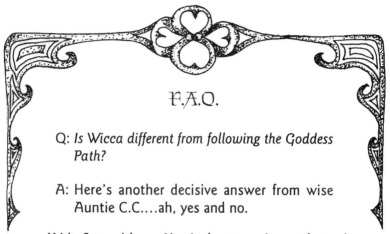

F.A.Q.

Q: *Is Wicca different from following the Goddess Path?*

A: Here's another decisive answer from wise Auntie C.C....ah, yes and no.

Wait. Stay with me. Here's the scoop. It was the ancient women healers, herbalists, diviners, and midwives who were the first to be branded as "witches" and singled out for persecution or, in many cases, cruel torture and death. It is estimated that more than a million women were executed between 1300 and 1600 for practicing their inherited folk beliefs, or tending to the medical needs of other women. The survivors were considered outlaws and heretics so they had to go underground—naturally, who wouldn't?—but many continued to communicate their knowledge in secret.

Centuries later, many of the original beliefs re-emerged with various interpretations, organized under the broad banner of Wicca. Unfortunately, as with all organized institutions, there were varying rules of conduct or conflicts of leadership. But, by and large, Wiccan beliefs are based on key elements from the folk traditions of the Celtic Clans who followed the Goddess. The practice of Wicca is simply more organized, with a community of adherents, a leadership hierarchy, and various rules of ritual and conduct.

If you consider Wicca, I advise you to research it carefully and choose one of the particular streams of thought and practice that most closely aligns with your own beliefs. In Wicca, magick often takes the form of a group dynamic with all the accompanying ups and downs of any group. On the plus side, it offers ready sisterhood and kindred thinking, and that may work for you. But no worries. The Clan Mothers believed in your right to exercise "free will." If you chose to go the way of organized Wicca, the Goddess will still remain central to your beliefs and to the course of your wondrous life.

But there is an alternative route to the same goal. Joining a coven isn't necessary and, for many of us, the horror of the persecutions by association still lingers deep within our bones and makes us a bit uneasy with public display. Call it a remnant of collective memory. Who knows? My family always urged caution, so it may have been handled down from some dreaded ancient experience.

As a young woman, you also have the choice to follow what is often called the "solitary Path," or the "self-initiatory way." That simply means, do it on your own. You learn on your own or with a trusted friend or mentor. The early Clan Wisewomen and Elders didn't require any special membership. You were simply born to it. But they did encourage women to be strong, self-confident, self-sufficient, kindly, and keenly in touch with their own magickal and healing powers. You can have all that as a solitary.

Traditionally, solitary followers of the Goddess were called "Hedge-Witches." Did that mean hiding behind a bush to cast your spell? Almost. It really referred to witches who couldn't practice their healing in public anymore. The story goes that they had to meet their clients out of sight, often in small, secret rooms hewn out of the thick bramble hedges that lined the roads. Sometimes, it is said, illegal classes were held in these same open rooms, so the master of the estate wouldn't know that the peasant children were learning. To be a hedge witch, continuing what you believe in, no matter the obstacles placed in your way, is an admirable Path to walk.

chapter 9

Give Guilt the Bum's Rush

Guilt. More guilt. Heap it on. Every day. Every way. It's a woman's heavy millstone, a painful burden, a constant sorrow. And worse, it is internal and completely invisible, a self-inflicted wound to your soul.

We are all riddled with guilt no matter the cause, the issue, or the person involved. You probably started young, and you have a greater capacity for shouldering guilt every year, don't you? *Heap more on, I can take it.* You probably learned about guilt from adult women in your life. They are trained experts. And like the perfect little mimics we are as children, you picked up all the subtleties, all the skill of turning blame back on yourself, whether valid or not. Even as you read this, a sense of guilt lurks just below the surface of your emotions, unbalancing you and causing anxiety, depression, maybe even panic attacks. Why do we do this to ourselves?

What causes guilt? Just about everything, I'd bet. Maybe you went out last night when you should have studied and now you feel, yep, guilty. Maybe you lied about something to keep the peace and that caused even more problems. Man, do you feel crummy about that, too. Or your parents split and it has to be your fault. That's wrong, but you can't see that. Or maybe yesterday you blew off some nasty comment and it was carried straight to the person who was, naturally, deeply wounded by what you said. Ugh! I hate when that happens! Now you feel rotten and the guilt is almost making you sick—at least sick at heart. I know. I've been there.

Women's guilt is centuries old, so your Clan Mothers learned ways to deal with it effectively. I warn you, they hate the suffering guilt causes you, my Spiritual Seeker. They'd say it's high time to **unlearn** that bad habit. Time to lighten up. Time to let your soul breathe. They would tell you this: Guilt has a limited time span of goodness. *Goodness?* Yes, guilt serves as a highly effective internal alarm that alerts you to the fact you've unknowingly stepped over the line, you've tripped up some-how, you've left the Goddess Path and stumbled over an ant-hill. Guilt's job is to scream inside your mind that you've broken a code, hurt a person's feelings, or done something you now realize you really shouldn't have done.

But get clear on this: The moral alarm bell is where guilt's value begins, and where it should end. Guilt is a gift, but it's stale-dated. A "Best Before" date should be printed right on the side. Then, you smart cookie, show it the door.

The real harm is done when you ignore the fact that guilt simply needs to be heard, and then it must be released. Instead, you continue to add the new guilt to all the old baggage you've accumulated, and then you haul it all around with you wher-ever you go. You're never free of it. That is…until now!

The Clan Mothers tell you that allowing the pain of guilt to hang around and continue to hurt you is a self-indulgent and cowardly reaction to what you've done. Look at it as a misplaced attempt to remedy the mistake you made by inflicting pain on yourself. You are trying to balance the pain you caused, by feel-ing pain. Hey! you may have invented a complicated math for-mula but, sorry, you lose—it doesn't prove out. Carrying hidden guilt deep inside is psychologically crippling and gets in the way of good soul work. It undermines self-confidence. It's a yucky, spit-out thing. Truth is: Guilt sucks.

Instead, start to approach the problem of guilt completely differently. Twirl yourself around. Get a fresh perspective. First, give your guilt some credit for whacking you upside the head so you could realize you did wrong. Period. It has no other value. Be grateful. Say to your guilt: *"Thanks for that, I hadn't realized until you stabbed me, that I really shouldn't have...."*

Good. You got the message. Yeah, you made a mistake. Now you fully realize it. So what's next? The Goddess way is to learn the fine art of "fair restitution," of making things better and atoning for the injury you caused by doing something about it. Taking good forthright action. Fair restitution means you fix your mistake as best you can. Patch it up. Kiss it better. Then let the useless, leftover guilt go. Let it vanish into thin air. *Poof.*

Believe me, the very act of trying to make amends is good soul work because you learn so much about yourself. Once you begin to practice this good deed, you'll never stop, because restitution releases the harmful guilt from your soul—it is pure emotional magick. It is an essential part of learning to walk the Goddess Path and it is well worth the trouble.

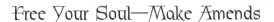

Free Your Soul—Make Amends

How do you release your guilt? We know that hurtful words can never be taken back, the pain has been inflicted. The arrow found its target. But you can learn from your mistakes, apply a little cosmic first aid, and let your guilt go.

But Auntie, if I didn't feel guilty,
I'd be an uncaring and terrible person.

No, not at all. Guilt doesn't make you better in any way. It depletes your life force. What makes you a caring person is the honest acceptance of responsibility for your wrongful act, your slip of the tongue, your questionable lifestyle that may be bringing grief to someone else. Once you accept that responsibility, you need to go further and take swift and meaningful Goddess action to repair and mend the pain you may have caused. Making amends, accepting blame if it truly is yours, apologizing: these make you a caring person. And a whole one to boot.

The simple truth is that no one, no matter how well-intentioned, can move through a lifetime on Abred without bumping into other people's feelings, stepping on toes, or accidentally causing pain. It is regrettable, but it can't be helped sometimes. We all do it. And occasionally we all act "without thinking." That's a given. But do we have to beat ourselves up day and night for a mistake we made? No, that's counterproductive.

Here's how to start down the liberating path of acting with fair restitution. Take a good look at all the burdens of guilt you carry around. Sort them out, one by one. Then decide what redress you can make, or what would be an appropriate expression of regret to the harmed party. The Clan Mothers caution you always to consider the person you have wronged when designing your act of fair restitution. Do nothing that could possibly bother or upset them further. Be aware of and sensitive to their feelings. You don't want to open old wounds or hurt them again, do you?

What sort of action on your part is appropriate? Consider writing a note of apology with no strings attached. Mail it or e-mail it. Then forget it and expect nothing in return. Send flowers or a small gift. In some cases, consider picking up the phone and calling. If your simmering guilt has roots from long ago, you may have to visit a graveside to whisper your words of repentance to the spirit of the departed. What else? Maybe you need to return money or borrowed clothes. Do it or at least make arrangements to do it through a third party. If something can't be changed, turned back, or amended, then quietly ask for forgiveness in your soul. You'll know the right action to take in each case.

Just keep in mind that this exercise is designed to unburden your conscience and make more room in your soul for joy, so it is imperative that you expect nothing from others in return. If you are hoping for a "thank you" or a pat on the back, you are putting strings of expectation on your fair restitution and you are setting yourself up for disappointment, further misunderstandings, and—need I say it?—more guilt. Keep your acts of restitution simple, unadorned, and unencumbered. After you have summoned up the courage and made your amends, it is time to turn to the task of mending yourself.

Follow your act of restitution with this simple spell. Set the stage by putting on your Lorica and follow all the necessary steps you now have mastered for good spellcasting.

Spell to Lift Guilt

In addition to your preparations, light a white candle and set it before you. Stare into the flame as you think back over what you have done to make amends, but don't let emotions intrude on your visualization. After you've "seen with your mind" each act of restitution, imagine your guilt around that issue. See it as a big black plastic bag with heavy, sloppy goop inside. It is draped over your shoulders, weighing you down. Now release your burden of guilt. See the imagined black bag of guilt slowly slide off your shoulders and plop in a heap on the ground. Then see it disappear. Gone. Repeat with each incident, if necessary. Now you are ready for the spell.

Take three deep breaths. Look into the candle flame, then snap your fingers in front of it and say:

> **Mother Mine, be by my side as I declare:**
> **In accordance with the Old Ways**
> **I have made fair restitution for my mistakes**
> **Take the burden of guilt from my soul**
> **Refresh my soul with insight and knowing**
> **Fill my soul with light, love, and newfound peace.**
>
> **Grant that I am unburdened**
> **Grant that I am free**
> **Blessed by Three**
> **Blessed Be.**

Snap you fingers once more before the flame. Place the burning candle in a safe place, such as the deep kitchen sink, and let it burn out. Your guilt has burned away, too. Vanished. You are free.

And if, by chance, the self-inflicted guilt should creep back into your thoughts, use your physical trigger. Snap your fingers in front of your face to remind yourself that the guilt has been treated with fair restitution and the Goddess has removed its burden. Then picture a beautiful natural setting, a place you love, and let your mind go there. It may take a bit of practice to totally transform the old guilt habit. Old habits can be stubborn.

But promise me that the next time you make a mistake, and you will, clear it up immediately. Don't suffer, my apprentice. Take rightful responsibility for your actions, make appropriate amends, and the pain caused by enduring lingering guilt will no longer be part of your sweet life.

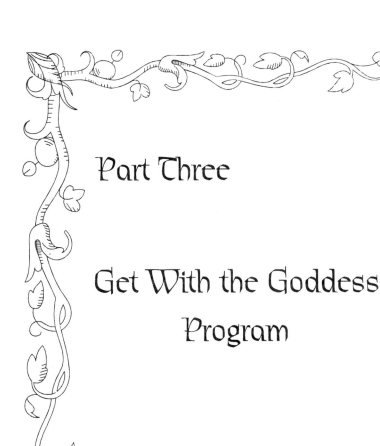

Part Three

Get With the Goddess Program

chApτeR 10

Yummy τhings to Learn About Your Soul

A huge part of any magickal kit bag is made up of knowledge. As an apprentice on the Goddess Path, you need to bone
up on everything to do with the ancient ways—the customs, the
festivals, and the annual rituals. In short, you need to know
your Goddess stuff. You need to talk your walk.

Getting familiar with the basics of everyday celebrations of
the Goddess is part of your overall training. Call it *Goddess
History 101,* but it is time for you to go to Soul School to research and learn the traditions of your journey. As a Spiritual
Seeker, take the time to get "filled in" on Goddess culture so
you never ever feel that you are lacking in knowledge of its
traditions in any way.

But don't sweat it. It's easy to learn the rhythms of the Goddess calendar. All the festivals add up to what was known as the
Great Celtic Wheel of the Year. To get familiar with them, you
only need to alter your thinking about holidays and begin to understand where many of our calendar events actually come from,
and what they really mean to you as an apprentice.

For instance, Halloween is a Goddess festival that has survived the centuries. The name is a contraction of All Hallows' Eve, which is the night before All Souls' or All Hallows' Day, but this night originally belonged to the Goddess Clan and was officially the eve of "Samhain" (pronounced Sow-in), which was a most important night. The modern world has kept the ghost-haunting traditions of Samhain or Halloween without the serious spiritual significance of the occasion. For you and me (think witch costumes with black cone hats), Samhain night marks the extra day of the year, the left over one that you've probably heard about in the old saying "a year and a day." What does that mean? Samhain was the extra day held separate from the others because it was, quite frankly, rather spooky. It was a day for the dead.

Samhain was a night set aside for the spirits to visit (now think ghost and goblin costumes). They were the spirits of your ancestors, friends, or, worse yet, your former enemies. The Celts believed these spirits walked out and among the people of the tribe on the eve of Samhain. Yikes!

But it wasn't all creepy like that of a horror movie set. Not at all. Samhain was very spiritual in nature. The Clan Mothers believed that it was the night when the veil was very thin between the world of those still living and the spirit world (Abred and the Otherworld), so thin as to be almost invisible. It was a time of prayer and renewal.

For you and me, Samhain can be a night of joyful reunion with the spirit of a loved one, or you might encounter a challenging trickster who plays with your intellect and perhaps threatens your safety (This is the "trick or treat" part that has survived). Depending on what spirits the Celts expected to call, Samhain could be pleasant or frightening. If they were worried about the return of a soul they had seriously wronged in the past, then Samhain could be so scary that doors were bolted shut and windows covered. You see, it pays to be good to people while they are still alive!

But Samhain was only one festival, or sacred Sabbat. Just looking at the list of events and festivities, feasts, ceremonies, and rounds of parties, you soon realize the followers of the Celtic Goddess were social beings and very busy. There are many festivals that they celebrate to this day: the four Equinoxes, the four seasonal Solstices, and the all-important Fire Holidays. Get familiar with the dates of the most important Sabbats so they begin to become part of your celebrations as well.

I'll tell you the dates and how to pronounce the Celtic names, but you'll need to do more work on this. Put on your research cap and find a book that tells you more about each festivity, so you can custom design your celebration rituals to reflect the meaning of each sacred event that comes down to you from antiquity. A good reference to try is Lady Sabrina's *Celebrating Wiccan Spirituality* (New Page Books, 2002). The Goddess loves ritual. She loves to party. She taught apprentices that enjoying all that life has to offer is an indication of a time well spent on Abred. Enjoy.

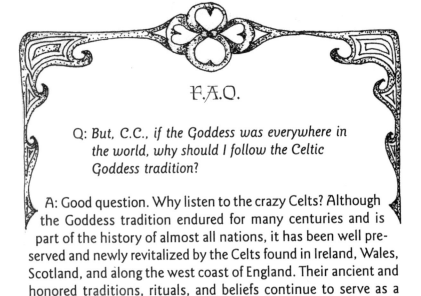

F.A.Q.

Q: But, C.C., if the Goddess was everywhere in the world, why should I follow the Celtic Goddess tradition?

A: Good question. Why listen to the crazy Celts? Although the Goddess tradition endured for many centuries and is part of the history of almost all nations, it has been well preserved and newly revitalized by the Celts found in Ireland, Wales, Scotland, and along the west coast of England. Their ancient and honored traditions, rituals, and beliefs continue to serve as a kind of cosmic computer data bank that's been kept full of valuable information and history.

Even through the centuries of the horrific witch burnings, many Celts remained steadfast in their adherence to the Goddess traditions, and the liberating principles of the feminine divine. Despite persecution, they continued to foster the Goddess values, rituals, and beliefs taught by their female ancestors and handed down, often secretly and with fear of punishment, from mother to daughter. Though much has changed through time, the Celtic Goddess tradition from the British Isles still provides a most reliable map for that extreme, off-road adventure called your life.

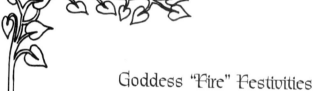

Goddess "Fire" Festivities

Of all the beloved or fun-loving festivities, the Clan Mothers placed the most emphasis on the "Fire holidays" that marked the midpoints between the Equinox and Solstice dates. The Fire holidays held great significance because the Great Mother Brigantia or Brigit (as she is called in Ireland) was the Goddess of a woman's hearth, or the Fire Goddess. They are: **Samhain, Imbolc, Beltain,** and **Lammas** or Lughnasadh. They marked the progress of Goddess creation and bounty expressed through agriculture's seeding times (rebirth), to harvesting times (death and abundance), as well as the birthing of domestic and wild animals. The Fire holidays were based on the cycles of nature and reinforced the Celtic concepts of birth, death, and regeneration, so the celebration of these festivals was a conscious reminder of the principles of the faith, of the Goddess Way. It kept the faith alive and thriving.

As you learn more about the meaning of each festivity, you will develop your own personal way of celebrating the Goddess within you and the significance of each particular event. You, too, will be reminded on a regular basis of just how special you are.

How to Pronounce Your Festivals with a Goddess Twang

If you want to strut your stuff a bit and sound as though you really know what you're talking about, then try to learn some of the Celtic or Gaelic pronunciations for these sacred Goddess events. It is sure to impress the crowds around you; it still impresses me! I already mentioned the fall festival called Samhain. Here's more info on all four fire holidays that are now yours to celebrate:

- **Samhain** (October 31). Pronounced "Sow-in" with emphasis on the "Sow" part. (Although in parts of Europe saying Sam-hane is perfectly acceptable.)

- **Imbolg** (February 2). Pronounced "Emm-bol-ug" with emphasis on the first syllable.

- **Beltain** (April 30/May 1). Pronounced mostly Bel-tane everywhere now. (An early version was B'yol-tinna with emphasis on the second syllable, but that's just Goddess trivia now.)

- **Lughnasadh**, or **Lammas** (August 1). The true pronunciation is Loo-na-sa with emphasis on the "Loo" part, like the name Hugh; but most people (me included) use **Lammas** which is pronounced Lam-es. Suit yourself, you accomplished apprentice, it's your spiritual vocabulary now.

CHAPTER 11

How Can There Be a Goddess Inside Me?

The concept of a deity dwelling within a walking, talking human being, is foreign to many teens. Why? Because the current religions on Abred teach that the deity is separate from humans and is found above or outside them. This is not necessarily a good thing. Because God is distant and essentially unknowable, such religions require someone to interpret God's feelings and intentions on a regular basis: Is God happy? Sad? Angry with us? They ultimately diminish the role of an individual's or group's responsibility for its actions. Let's face it, is a "holy war" really God's idea?

So, what about a Goddess within? Is this such a strange idea? Both male and female Celts followed the teachings of the Goddess and believed that She was part of each and every living being. And because following the Goddess was not a faith that separated religion from daily life, the early Celts looked to the everyday workings of their world to witness the daily presence of the Goddess. And where did they find the clearest indication of the Goddess at work? They found it within the women of the clan.

It couldn't be overlooked that women, alone, had the awesome ability to create life through the act of birth, just as the Goddess gave birth to all that was living on the earth plane. The men watched as their wives, mothers, sisters, aunts, and female cousins moved naturally through the three phases of the Goddess: maiden, then mother, and finally the old, but revered, crone. As with the Goddess, so it was with women.

On the practical side of tribal life, women oversaw all the acts that were thought to be Goddess related. Women were in charge of healing the sick, birthing and assisting at the births of humans and animals, laying out the dead, divining the future, conjuring and working magick, as well as presiding at and leading the sacred rituals and ceremonies that paid tribute to the Goddess. It was clear that a human woman and the Goddess were kindred, interrelated, and therefore, logically and spiritually inseparable—one from the other. The Goddess and woman are one.

So too, are you, one with the Goddess within you.

When your mind accepts the truth that the Goddess dwells within your heart and soul, you feel uplifted and transported. You are whole. You are divine. You straddle this world and the Otherworld. You are spiritually infused. And you begin to live a belief, a fundamental faith, that was shared by men and women for untold centuries all over the world. You reconnect with a rich and sustaining faith that has been described as "the faith of human eternity."

You are a creative and intuitive young woman who knows there is more to life than that which meets the eye. You are right. You are drawn to the Goddess Path because it rings true in your soul. You want to use your magickal gifts to heal, to fix, to cure, to draw the positive, to create the light and to make life—yours and that of your friends and family—better.

So, my Spiritual Seeker, it is not a long leap of faith from here to the eternal and immortal truth: You and the Goddess are One. Accept it. It's true. It is beautiful. It is the way to live life at your very best.

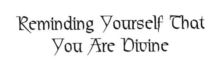

Reminding Yourself That You Are Divine

Goddess followers soon learn that personal affirmations are a surefire way to remind yourself of all your earthly and spiritual blessings, gifts, and magick. They are also a way of calling up healing or positive change, and good fortune.

The strength of affirmations is not based on force and intensity like other magick spells, but rather through repetition. Success and positive energy is called forth by the rhythm and cadence of sound. Unlike more commanding spells, affirmations can be said quietly, under your breath, and often are. Affirmations are comforting and reassuring. Yippee, yippee! They really work!

As you did with the self-blessing chant, you can write your own affirmations. Just include a clear statement as in the following example written by Sirona Knight.

First, let me tell you a bit about Sirona Knight. She is an amazing woman, skilled and highly accomplished in the ancient mysteries, yet she remains totally warm and approachable. Her first name means *Morning Star* in Gaelic, and by her actions I consider her to be a true Clan Mother to all of us. She works diligently through her many books to bring light to our world, a bright and shining light. In her book **Goddess Bless!** (Red Wheel Press), Sirona offers this awesome affirmation to remind you of the beauty and power that is shared by you and the Goddess. Learn it. Say it every day. It is a sacred reminder of just how terrific you are.

Maiden Magick

I am awakening the divine power of the Goddess
within me,
every moment of every day.

Mother Goddess, full of grace, I celebrate your love.

My heart is the heart of the Goddess.
My heart is open.

My eyes are the eyes of the Goddess.
My eyes are open.

My soul is the soul of the Goddess.
My soul is divine.

We are One.

—Sirona Knight, *Goddess Bless!*

chapter 12

Create a Sacred Calendar, and Where's the Next Party?

Ha! Did you do a double take when you saw the title? Did you think,

Auntie C.C.! Have you no respect?
Worship and parties? Did my spiritual teacher
just say to pop the sacred and the profane in the
same blender and whir up a wild cosmic cocktail?
No way!

Yes way, as my wee friend, Seamus, used to say. Following up sacred Goddess ritual with merrymaking is based on centuries of tradition. You see, the crafty Clan Mothers were rather cool and hip women by today's standards. They were wise community leaders and very well connected to the wonders of the cosmic world, yet they loved a good time. They loved to dress up, wear makeup, and color their hair with reds and purples and greens. They wanted a different hairstyle for every festival, and they'd spend hours doing each other up for the party. They were the *It* girls of the Celtic Clans!

Before a Sabbat, the Clan Mothers cooked up a storm to make sure they had plenty of food for the party afterwards. And they instructed the Brew Mother to prepare big batches of mead, their golden honey wine, and barrels of herb-flavored beers. Then they sent out a call, sometimes to other tribes, to hire great musicians, storytellers, comedians, and even puppeteers.

On the night of the celebration, when all the traditions of faith had been observed, and the Goddess properly praised and revered—the good times rolled. Everyone brought their braziers to the edge of the bonfires to barbecue fresh venison steaks, or ribs of wild boar. When everyone had their fill, the music would start up and the dancing would break out. Don't you just love bonfire parties in the country? Well, you come by it naturally, dear apprentice. This is your Goddess history. It's probably etched on your cellular makeup.

Of course, you can't take away from the fact that all the early Celts were deeply spiritual in their love and observation of the Goddess—just like you and me—but, man, did they love to celebrate. To them it was part of the homage to the Great Mother. They believed that all they received on Abred, including food and drink and the talent of entertainers, were gifts given directly from the Goddess. Laughter, dancing, singing, flirting, and merrymaking of all kinds (as long as it hurt no one) was an integral part of their faith; part of their duty to Her, to enjoy all that She had provided.

And you can bet your boots every party ran on high emotions. It wasn't unusual to see crying one minute, after a sad tale or legend of loss, and robust laughter the next. Tears and laughter were the standard fare for all good times. Honestly, have you ever been to a big blow-out party where there wasn't at least one person crying before the night was out? It's all part of the great emotional stew of living life to the fullest.

Just one word of caution: Party times should be good fun times. It's essential that no one is harmed through your merry-making. But be clear on this: Never drink and drive, nor condon violence or disrespect for others. If you are coming from that strong, positive place within yourself, and you observe safety and caution with diligence, then the Goddess says, "Go ahead, enjoy all that I have made for you, all the beauty that life on Abred has to offer." Including laughter and fun in your life is to walk the Goddess Path.

Write This Down!
Goddess Rituals and
Parties

Start by studying the Fire holidays. Make them special in your life by honoring them with some little ritual that you read about, or that you invent (the best kind).

Then consider the four major seasonal changes: the Winter and Summer Solstices that mark the often abrupt shift of the seasons; and the Spring and Autumn Equinoxes, because they mark more than just a temperature change. I'm thinking of the natural pull you feel in your body each Spring as it wants to break out after a cold Winter; or how you naturally want to slow down and add a few pounds as the Autumn days shorten and darken down. The Solstice and Equinox festivals celebrate important days of Earthly transition; sacred days that mark the change in hours of light and weather; the thinning or the thickening of your blood; or even that undeniable pull to romance. They clearly signify the cycles of the Goddess: birth, death, and regeneration.

Most importantly, bring your apprentice curiosity and your pure intent to witness and take part in the celebrations. Be your true self and don't forget your party clothes!

We begin with the Fire holidays—the most sacred in my mind—but all those listed are Sabbats. Various traditions put different emphasis on different days, or celebrate many others. All are correct, of course. No worries. There can never be too much celebrating. The Sabbats begin at sunset and carry on through to sunrise the next day.

Sunset marked the beginning of each day for the Celts, because the Mother Moon sky was their measuring stick, their calendar, their timepiece. That is why there are two dates shown for each festive day, as they begin at nightfall. It is like Halloween where the kids don't go prowling the neighborhoods in their costumes until after dark, even today.

- ☉ Samhain   31 October–01 November
  Feast of the spirits (first day of year)
- ☉ Imbolg   01–02 February
  Brigit's Day (Great Mother's Day)
- ☉ Beltane   30 April–May 01
  Fire festival (Renewed Life, Love)
- ☉ Lammas   31 July–01 August
  Corn harvest (Appreciation)

Solstices:

Winter Solstice (Yule celebration)
20–21 December

Summer Solstice (Midsummer festival)
21–22 June

Equinoxes:

Spring Equinox (Alban Eilir Celebration)
20–21 March

Autumn Equinox (Alban Elfed Celebration)
September 20–21

Throw a Great Pumpkin Party

Samhain, despite its bad press, can be a positive and enriching celebration under your direction. Traditionally, the candle inside the jack-o'-lantern represents the duality of a kindly welcome and a scary warning. The pumpkin is carved in a grotesque way to drive away unwanted tricksters, while the candle glowing inside it is meant to welcome the beloved and benevolent spirits. Samhain is a lovely time to have a quiet ceremony, and a great costume (or shapeshifting) party afterwards.

Be sure to cast your Lorica with a strong light of protection around you and your friends before you begin.

If you already have a carved pumpkin, it is doing its spiritual work. Place it (or them) in your Samhain Circle. In addition, you and your friends may wish to make a further welcome to the goodly spirits by placing a pottery (or wooden) bowl with salt in it just below the surface of the soil. This digging beneath the level of the earth symbolizes all that is unseen but is still with us. (If the ground is frozen, don't worry about the digging part.) Stand a white candle in the salt in the bowl and light it, clearly speaking out your loved one's name from the other side, along with a few kind words. This indicates to those of the Otherworld that you are surrounding yourself with spirit energy that is loving and positive, healing and helpful. If each of you in the group has someone to commemorate, have a bowl of salt and a candle for each and have them speak out the name and say some loving words about that spirit.

If you do this indoors, even the act of lighting a white candle and dedicating it to loving ancestors or friends who have crossed over will do. After the declaration, set the candle or candles in your window as a sign of welcome, it will be a strong gesture that is sure to draw only the good spirits and beautiful blessings.

After the ceremony, put on your costume, break open the orange drinks and the black candy and have some fun. Tell me now, will the way you think of Halloween ever be the same for you? Will life be? Not likely.

Have a great pumpkin party.

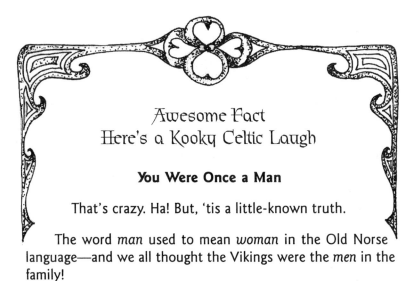

Awesome Fact
Here's a Kooky Celtic Laugh

You Were Once a Man

That's crazy. Ha! But, 'tis a little-known truth.

The word *man* used to mean *woman* in the Old Norse language—and we all thought the Vikings were the *men* in the family!

Actually, the name *man* meant *Moon* in Old Norse and among the other tribes in Europe. The early European tribes believed the moon was feminine—Mother Moon—and that She was the creator of all creatures. So a *woman* was a *man*, cross-culturally speaking. Consequently, The Isle of Man off Britain's coast was once sacred to—you guessed it—the Moon Goddess.

Okay. If that's so, then what the heck were men *called?*

Well, the word that we know as *man* today was originally *wer* from the Sanskrit root *vir*, which means, of course, that a *werewolf* is a *man-wolf.* And let's face it, after a bad romance day, don't you think there might just be a shred of truth in that wee fact!

—Information gleaned from *The Woman's Encyclopedia of Myths and Secrets*, Barbara G. Walker, Harper Collins, 1983

Part Four

Embracing Spiritual Commitment

CHAPTER 13

The Importance of Ritual

Using ritual to draw the heavenly spirits is as old a tradition as life itself. It is an essential spiritual act in all faiths, in all religious observances, great and small, worldwide. By repeating sounds and movements, and by using specially designated props in the ritual, you infuse each action, sound, or song with deep memories and lofty meaning.

The simple act of ritual marks a change, a shift in consciousness. It jogs your brain into thinking beyond everyday life. Just beginning a ritual that you are familiar with and know by heart serves to raise you up and beyond the weight of everyday pettiness, worry, and constant struggle. It gives you a real and dependable "time out" from all the thinking that drags you down, saps your energy, and crushes your hope. Ritual can be thought of as a great sigh of relief from your soul.

When a ritual begins, we are also alerted on another level. It says, "Hey, wake up! Pay attention to your spiritual life"— your soul work. Ritual is often beautiful and it is always comforting. All in all, ritual is pretty neat.

Dr. Clarissa Pinkola Estes, the wondrous Clan Mother who wrote that sign-post book, *Women Who Run with the Wolves*

(Ballantine Books), says this about the importance of ritual: "Ritual is one of the ways in which humans put their lives in perspective, whether it be Purim, Advent or drawing down the moon. Ritual calls together the shades and specters in people's lives, sorts them out, puts them to rest."

It's interesting to think about all the nonreligious ritual in your daily life—family ritual and little personal quirks of behavior. Maybe you have a special coffee cup that you reach for every time and you are convinced with each swallow that the bitter brew tastes better in that particular cup. Or perhaps you have a seat at the kitchen table that is always yours and it feels weird when you have to sit somewhere else. Even the family gathering at the table is a ritual. It signals a time set aside for each other, no matter what is going on in your relationships. Christmas holidays are full of family rituals, or rituals you've invented with your friends around gift-giving or shopping. We find comfort in ritual.

Casting your Lorica of protection, conjuring spells, doing daily affirmations, and blessing friends and loved ones are ritualistic in nature, but it takes tools or a designated special place to really nail it all down and focus your spiritual energy.

An altar is such a special place. Every church, temple, mosque, shrine, or ashram seems to have one, doesn't it? There is a certain change in the tempo of our thoughts and emotions whenever we approach an altar, even if the religion isn't our own: A certain awe or a kind of peace and reverence.

Maybe an altar would help focus your spiritual awakening, your calling up of the sustaining comfort of the feminine divine, your Goddess energy. An altar can be a fun project that will give you everything we've talked about: a place to do your own rituals; a place of spiritual expansion, peace, and focus; a place to use consecrated tools and talismans; a place that signals you are about to call up the Forces of Good to be with you, to comfort you. An altar is a place of your own.

Build an Altar,
Furnish It With Groovy Talismans

The Goddess faith is totally portable—wireless and mobile. It is beyond the latest technology, yet entirely natural and ancient in every good way.

Now, after singing the praises of altars, I'll really confuse you because you don't really need an altar of any kind. In fact, you may give some thought as to whether you want to expose your innermost thoughts and actions to others by having a place set aside for rituals—a place they can see, or comment upon, or even object to in some way. That's the argument for not building an altar. The "con" side. I've said it: You don't need one.

But, hey, maybe you want one. And just the desire for one may be enough reason to do it. That's the "pro" side. If that is so, let's imagine it into being. Build it or keep it in your mind—it's the same thing.

If you want a "real" one, start thinking about where it might be and decide what neat things you want to put into it. It could be up in your bedroom or in a corner of the attic. If privacy is a concern, consider making your altar in a secret place outdoors. It would be natural to build your altar, your special place to talk with the Goddess and draw up your full spiritual energy, right out in the woods, or in a meadow, or on a beach. But that's not always readily available, or possible.

Traditionally, the Great Mother Brigit, the Fire Goddess, was worshipped at the kitchen hearth and outside at the blazing bonfires and campfires—not so easy to find nowadays, and I don't suppose a microwave oven or a barbecue makes much of a substitute. The Earth, the world around us, is the body of the Goddess. To walk in the woods, or simply to find peace in the great outdoors, is to be enfolded by Her. Maybe there's a park or a garden near you?

Inside or outside, in either case, there are no rules. How do you start? If you want to set up an altar outside, get some big stones and pile them up to your liking. Decorate the altar with herbs, specials rocks, and pieces of bark or shells or feathers. Things that speak to you. Talismans.

What are they? Talismans are any object that you infuse with special energy and abilities. They hold onto your energy and incorporate your specific instructions. So, they may be "lucky" or "healing," or they may serve as an opening channel to the Goddess. When you call on your talismans, they obey by radiating back exactly what you charged them to do. They are your ready servants. Talismans can be rocks, or a rabbit foot, dried leaves, semiprecious stones, shells, rings, feathers, or anything you choose. They can be carried with you or left at your altar. Talismans are great Goddess medicine. They speak to your subconscious and make good things happen.

Sanctifying your Goddess altar

As we discussed, altars are a conduit to the sacred, so they need respect. When you are finished building it, however simple or elaborate it may be, you must formally sanctify your altar. Start by lighting a small (safe) candle. (Be sure to have water on hand). Invite the spirits of the four cardinal points of North, East, South, and West to lend their blessings, and include the spirits represented by the Elements of Air, Water, Fire, and Earth. Touch your fingers to your third eye to bring forward your Lorica of Protection, and see that misty white light surround you and the altar. Raise both hands to the heavens and say something such as this in your practiced, big spell-making voice:

**Great Mother Mine, creator of all I survey
and the One who dwells within my happy
soul,
I beg you come to this humble altar that your
apprentice has created for you alone.**

**Know that You are always as close to me as
my heartbeat, for we are One.**

**Thanks be for your many blessings in my life
and the gifts You have bestowed upon me.**

**Help me as I work diligently to reach my full
potential.**

**This altar of spiritual love and everlasting
gratitude is an expression of my heart.**

Join me here among the Forces of Good.

**I dedicate this altar before me
exclusively to you.
Show me the way.
Blessed by Three.**

Blessed Be.

There, you now have a sanctified altar on which to carry out
your rituals. It is your own special blessed place, wherever you
have built it, even if it is only in your imagination. Well done.

chapter 14

Self-Initiation: Yikes! Am I Ready?

You betcha! It's time to take a giant step outside your everyday mind. Just grab hold of your wondrous spiritual gifts with all the magick and mystery they represent. The Self-Initiation is empowering. It's fun. And with your Lorica—your Spell of Protection—you're safe as a cricket in the pocket of the Goddess. But before you step further, let's take stock of where you've been so far in this excellent adventure.

Time for your Goddess report card

Hey, I'm kidding. But you need to look at all you've learned and mastered so far on your Goddess Path. You'll be amazed, Spiritual Seeker, by what you've accomplished. You haven't "just passed," you're an honor student! Take a pen and check off the magickal feats on the following list, one by one. Wow! You've mastered 13 skills so far and, by the way, the number 13 is a very lucky number for you and me:

☐ You've picked up this book, embraced it, and begun to skip down your Goddess Path. That in itself is an awesome commitment.

☐ You've let me, your Celtic Auntie C.C., walk along with you as your mentor. Together we conducted a little spell to feel the presence of your Clan Mothers.

☐ You've openly, and with impressive gusto, declared your intent to claim your rightful place of membership in the time-honored sisterhood of the Goddess.

☐ You've learned to "keen up" and make note of the signs and animal omens that cross your Path every day. More than that, you've begun to interpret what they mean.

☐ You've learned how to conjure up the all-important Lorica, your lifelong Spell of Protection, for the benefit of yourself and everyone you love and care about.

☐ You've taken time to pamper your neglected soul, and to acknowledge the importance of developing self-esteem and taking good care of yourself in the name of the Goddess through the ritual of Self-Blessing.

☐ You've learned the historic value of chants and you've gone even further and created your own. Wow!

☐ You've examined your personal needs and taken Goddess control of your life to shoulder more responsibility and become more independent. Your status in the tribe has risen since you began to walk the Goddess Path with such gutsy vigor.

☐ You've kissed off all the heavy guilt you carried; and you've experienced the value in the simple action of making amends to free your soul from burdens.

☐ You've charted a course of study by beginning to celebrate the Goddess calendar, by making note of the Sabbats and becoming familiar with Goddess history.

☐ You've learned to use affirmations to re-enforce your faith in yourself and the Goddess within. You've written them yourself and repeated them on the way to school to draw up your personal artillery of confidence and kindness.

☐ You've accepted that you have a birthright to fun and good times as an elemental part of the groovy Goddess way, just as your ancestors did in ancient times, as long as you stick to the code of "harming no one."

☐ You've recognized the benefits of ritual for concentrating your mind and practicing your faith; and you've built an altar filled with love and special talismans.

Whew! Now, *you tell me,* after stuffing all those 13 spiritual skills—those amazing accomplishments—into your own magickal kit bag, don't you think you're ready for the next exciting step (maybe the most exciting) in your spiritual quest?

Sure you are. You know it in your heart.

Claiming Your Maiden Magick

Well, my able Apprentice, I'd say you are definitely ready for your Initiation ritual. It's a sacred crossroads in your lifelong spiritual quest. Believe me, it's huge!

Read all this over in advance. Think about it, so your spiritual self can grow comfortably accustomed to the steps required to stage the Initiation and claim your magick. You can do your Initiation with a like-minded, trusted friend, or by yourself in a comfortable, safe environment. Either way, be assured that you are never alone. The kindly spirits are with you. I'm with you. Blessed Be, Magical Maiden, the Goddess smiles on you.

First, establish your solid foundation of Maiden Magick

This is an unassailable truth: Your personal storehouse of magick is found in your joyful experiences in life. This is simple, but absolutely true. We've all had our ups and downs and challenges in life, that is a given, but we've also been blessed with really happy moments when we thought we might fly from the sweet joy of it all. It was during these special times that you actually ducked under the loving wing of the Goddess, when She shared your happiness and smiled and laughed along with you. You temporarily stepped through the veil between the worlds—lifted by your burst of happiness.

Though you didn't realize it, you were building a unique stockpile of Goddess knowing, of spiritual strength, of magick. These very happy memories are the basis for conjuring magick and changing the world for the better. And the best news is that this magickal arsenal is yours alone, and it is powerful. Remembering and embracing all those blissful moments is a pivotal part of your Initiation ceremony.

How do you bring up this magickal Webpage of Goddess knowing again? Easy. Simply do this in advance of your Initiation:

Sit in a quiet place. Cast your Lorica by tapping your third eye. Visualize yourself wrapped in the misty light of protection and then recall one happy occasion in your past.

Bring up a scene from your own movie: a time when you were so happy, you'll never forget it. It may be an event, such as a family gathering when everyone you love was at their very best; or a time when you were praised by those you love; or it may be the first time your eyes locked with that handsome guy in the hall you were wild about. Maybe something terrific happened at a party; it may be that single hug when you needed it the most from someone you love. Okay...I bet you remember a whole slew of things.

You will need to relive each joyful memory before you lock it in with a physical trigger, so that its positive energy is captured and always on call to act as your solid base of Goddess magick.

Start with the first memory. Rerun it in your mind. Turn up the volume and the light. Feel the air, its temperature and humidity. In short, *be* there. Feel the absolute breadth of your happiness at that moment. Smile. This is pure joy.

Creating your sacred Power Fist

Now you will create a physical trigger to lock that pure energy in place so that, ever after, you'll be able to call up this moment of Goddess bliss. Pow! In an instant.

You have that happy memory in mind: vivid as laser light, sound cranked to the max. Then hold up your left hand, because it has always represented your spiritual and sacred side. Tuck the thumb against your palm and squeeze hard with your fingers. Ouch! Feel that? That's called your Power Fist.

Hold your arm out straight in front of you, give a quick squeeze of your Power Fist, and say:

Let this moment of bliss represent my own Goddess Magick.

Well done! This is your physical trigger for instant replay; for revisiting those wonderful moments when you were warmly hugged by the Goddess Herself. Ah, bliss.

Repeat with each of the magickal memories that are yours alone, until you have claimed each and every one. Then start up the band. Your soul is ready for its Self-Initiation.

Preparations for Your Initiation into the Goddess Way

Before you start: a few things for you to gather together.

1. You need to find and prepare a quiet place for your Self-Initiation. It will take about half an hour.

2. Get your heavenly bearings. What does that mean? If you don't already know (and few people keep track anymore), find out where North is so that you may look in that direction when you begin to call on the cardinal (compass point) spirits to attend.

3. Bring along a talisman that is special. A rock, a crystal, a piece of jewelry, a stuffed animal that is dear to you, or some small but treasured thing left to you by someone you love or who may have passed over to the other side. No hard rules here on what, or how many, to bring when you surround yourself with the power of love tokens.

4. Gather your representatives of the Celtic "Elements."

The Elements? What's that?

The Clan Mothers believed that there is strong spiritual medicine to be found within the natural Elements of this beautiful world. The Celts called them the Elements. There are five, like the points on the pentagram: Air, Water, Fire, Earth, and a lesser known fifth, called Ire, from the verb "to go." Some think of Ire as the vastness of the sky and raise their arms in welcome. I think of it as the lovely whisper of the Goddess on the wind.

I sometimes make the motion of touching my heart with my fingertips, then moving the fingers to my lips to blow a kiss, like a happy child to her smiling mother.

The Elements should always be present at your rituals, if possible, because their presence adds an extra and powerful "oomph." Choosing a representative of the Elements can be a lot of fun and the possibilities are limitless. A simple tea candle floating in a small bowl of water may symbolize the presence of both Fire and Water. Your own breath, used to blow softly on the flame to make it dance joyfully, could be counted as the presence of Air. Either a pinch of salt, a rock, or a tiny bit of garden soil are ideal symbols for Earth.

5. Create your magick kit bag. All Apprentices of the Goddess need to have, or make, a special container as a safe-keep for their magick ingredients. Just like all things magickal, it can be real or simply reside in your mind. How about a dark blue velvet bag with long golden cords, or a rough cardboard box with dried leaves and natural tendrils glued to it. Or you can buy something that catches your fancy, but whatever it is, it must be treated with reverence and cared for with sincere attention.

What goes into your kit bag? In addition to the candles and other symbols for the Elements, you might add any herbs and plants you collect to enhance the magickal process. The apprentices of antiquity placed all the new thoughts, all the freshly learned skills and acquired women's "knowing" into their kit bags. Think of Native American Medicine Bags that were revered as sacred far beyond their contents.

6. Prepare traditional wine and cakes. *Wine?* Well, maybe not, but at least bring its representative—grape juice—it's every bit as good. The Celts were strong believers in the necessity of enjoying life and celebrating every accomplishment—big or small—along life's journey.

As the Aunties used to say, got your kit 'n' gear? Then you are ready to begin.

This is It! Your Self-Initiation into the Goddess Way

Time to begin: Exhale your troubles

You have found somewhere quiet and peaceful—a place where you won't be disturbed. Inside the house is fine, but outside is great because this spell would be further enhanced by the attendance of the good spirits of Nature. Either is perfect.

Sit in a comfortable chair or on the grass. Have some mystical music playing, if you like. Cast your Lorica: Tap your fingers to your third eye three times and visualize the light of protection all around you.

Take three deep breaths, one for each phase of the Goddess Path, the three Women's Mysteries of Transformation that you are bound to know and experience in your long and full lifetime—the Maiden, the Mother, and the Crone. Use these three breaths to cleanse your soul as you did for the Lorica spell.

Honoring the Elements

Set representatives for the Elements around you. Pour the water in a bowl and whisper,

> **Wondrous gift of Water. Thanks be Great Mother.**

Float the tea candle in the water, light it and say,

> **Wondrous gift of Fire. Thanks be Great Mother.**

Lean over, softly blow on the candle, watch the flame dance and say,

Wondrous gift of Air. Thanks be Great Mother.

Pour your salt or soil in a little heap near you, and whisper,

Wondrous gift of Mother Earth. Blessed be.

For Ire, make a loving gesture—hug yourself or touch your fingers to your lips, it is up to you, and say,

Wondrous gift of joy in my spiritual progress and growth, Ire be blessed.

Now remember, the words are suggestions. All ritual is a private form of devotion and you should change or customize your tributes to suit yourself. There's no set rule, but do take the time to follow the steps of acknowledgment that I outlined.

Okay Auntie C.C. What's next?

Time to use that great trigger, the Goddess-conjuring gesture that calls up your personal Maiden Magick—your Power Fist. Hold it straight out before you at shoulder height. Look at it and state with real conviction:

Great Mother Mine, come nigh by me as I embark on my Self-Initiation with your blessing on my soul.

Let me know my gift of women's magick.

Hear me as I dedicate my life, my Goddess work and my own magick to the Forces of Good.

Blessed be.

Feel the power surge through you; feel your strong conviction. Give your thumb a hard squeeze as a physical reminder of these empowering sensations.

Lower your arm and relax. Breathe calmness into your soul and let out a long, low sigh. Feel the warmth and loving presence of your Goddess. She is with you in love and support.

Invite your helpers

Think for a moment. Do you have anyone on the other side, in the Otherworld; someone you loved and cherished who has died and gone on before you? Or a guardian angel or spirit guide you are sure watches over you? Well, now is the time to invite them to your ceremony. If you hold in your heart the love of a special ancestor, a lost friend, a faerie, a spirit guide, or a beloved pet dwelling happily in Avalon, then ask them to please come and be with you at this important initiation ceremony, to help make it stronger still. Picture them coming forward and sitting down at your side, then whisper,

Thanks be.

Cast your power Circle

Now is the time to cast the sacred Circle. This is a commencement ritual venerated through time and it is one that you will use often. There are a number of ways to do it. My Clan Mothers taught me to cast a golden circle of light in my mind. Within that light you will be able to draw on the Forces of Good—the amazing power of the Goddess—and you will be protected by that very energy.

Casting the Circle of light is just one way to mark the area for spiritual ritual. Many followers of the Old Way use a sacred tool, or the branch of a beloved tree, to actually draw a Power Circle on the ground around themselves or their group, walking clockwise for three complete revolutions. This is a dramatic way to define a sacred place and it, too, works great.

Summoning the Spirits of the Celtic Watchtowers

North, East, South, and West. What does each have to do with your initiation? Plenty. The Clan Mothers always included the awesome powers of the four cardinal or compass point spirits that they called the Watchtowers. To include these powerful but and kindly spirits is to pay ancient respect to the cycles of the universe.

Look first to the north, for the Clan Mothers recognized that the magnetic pull of the North Pole is strong magick. Stand as you welcome the spirits of the Watchtowers.

Greet each in turn with a nod and a smile and say:

> **Spirit of the North,**
> **blow energy cool and pure as fresh-fallen**
> **snow when you come by me,**
>
> **Welcome.**

Turn your body to the East, nod in recognition, and say:

> **Spirit of the East,**
> **bring forth the energy of a hopeful sunrise**
> **when you come by me.**
>
> **Welcome.**

Make a quarter turn to face the South and say,

> **Spirit of the South,**
> **fill my loving heart with your soothing**
> **warmth when you come by me.**
>
> **Welcome.**

Turn to the West and say,

> **Spirit of the West,**
> **cradle me gently as you do the setting sun,**
> **come by me.**
>
> **Welcome.**

Hold both your arms up high to the sky in greeting and say,

> **Great Mother Mine, beloved ones, friends,**
> **spirit helpers, sacred Elements and the spirits**
> **of the Watchtowers, thank you for lending me**
> **your strength as I step into my ritual of**
> **Initiation into the Goddess way.**
>
> **Stand by me now and always.**
>
> **Fortify me.**
>
> **Thanks be for your loving gifts.**

Initiation Oath

Good girl. You're doing excellent work. Now address the Goddess directly. It is time to make your declaration of Initiation. Squeeze your Power Fist and say:

> **Great Mother Mine, Goddess within me, You and I are One.**
>
> **Kindly look my way.**
>
> **Thrice bless me and guide me to expand my soul as a true and devoted Woman of Spirit;**
>
> **Guide me to better my world as I tread softly and surely as a confident Woman of Goodness;**
>
> **Guide me to believe in myself, my unique talents and my many gifts from You, and to use my woman's intuition, my sacred skills of crafting spells and conjuring healing as a blessed, beloved and devoted Woman of the Goddess that I am today, and will always be, from this beautiful day forward.**
>
> **So mote it, So it shall be.**
>
> **Blessed by Three.**
>
> **Blessed Be.**

Take a brief moment of shimmering silence to feel the surge of Goddess power within you. Ahh, it is beautiful. You have stepped forward and asked to be counted. You have turned the course of your future in the direction of Goodness and Light. You will achieve much good on your Goddess Path, and for that we are all grateful.

Closing the Circle and bidding fare thee well

One last little thing to do in your ritual. Formally bid goodbye and "thanks be" to all who helped and supported you in this important personal ceremony. First release the spirits of the Watchtower. But do so backwards. Start by facing North then turn one quarter left to the West and say,

Thanks be Spirit of the West for your assistance.

Fare thee well.

Repeat this same expression of appreciation to each of the compass points, finishing with the North. There! Each of the spirits has done its duty, you have honored its presence and they are now released to return to their place of power.

Now bid good-bye to your spirit helpers, loved ones, and friends. Nod and simply say,

Thanks be for each and every one for your help, Dear ones.

Fare thee well.

And lastly, pay tribute to the Goddess.

Great Mother Mine, thanks be for your kind and loving presence in my initiation and in my everyday life.

Stay by me.

Blessed be.

Beautiful. You are finished. Close your Circle. *How do I do that, C.C.?* Simple. Use the same method whether you cast the Circle of Light or you actually drew the sacred Circle around you. Pick up the stick or wand and walk in the opposite direction from the opening of the Circle, or imagine the Circle running back upon itself until it is erased. Whisper:

The Circle is closed. So be it.

Wow! You are initiated into the Goddess way. And you did it yourself, you wondrous creature. My hearty congratulations.

I hug you warmly, I whoop and shout, clap my hands and jump around in sheer delight. Feel me pat your shoulders for a job well done. How can you help but believe in yourself?

Cakes and wine: Party on down

I was wrong. There's one more thing to do: Party. You may get tired of me telling you to celebrate your accomplishments but it can't be helped parties are in my genes. Some people call it; "stopping to smell the roses." My Clan Mothers called it "Marking the passing pleasures of Abred." Call it what you will, part of the Goddess tradition—your tradition now—is to party-hearty while you are on earth and to honor good deeds with laughter and "kicking up your heels."

The party also clearly marks the end of the sacred interlude and your return to the "here and now." To the Clans, laughing, dancing, music, and general good fun bordered on the sacred. Granted, the Celtic ancestors sometimes went too far with the "demon drink" and that wasn't cool. Wasn't then, isn't today. But alcohol isn't the major ingredient—oh no—it is the frivolity, silliness, and good, crazy fun that you strive for after the hard work is done.

So break open the sweet cakes, and make a toast or two to the heavens with a wee dram of a bubbly substitute. Let yourself feel a warm wave of satisfaction for a job well done, for a lesson freshly learned and a skill newly acquired. You have good reason to party on down, you superstar, and count your many fine blessings. You deserve each and every one of them.

chapter 15

How to Use the Magick at Your Fingertips

Now that you have been initiated into the Goddess Way, you are no longer an apprentice. You have rightfully graduated to the ranks of an initiate and you can turn your hand to more magick, more good works. Your magick is as close to you as the squeeze of a hand, and you can soon begin to weave magick spells, blessings, and even healings with more relaxed confidence.

The steps are always the same. Before every spell, blessing, ritual, or ceremony, simply take a moment to focus your mind and activate your Goddess energy to influence the outcome of your rituals for the positive. Just learn these steps by heart and you won't even have to think twice:

1. Take three cleansing breaths.

2. Cast your Lorica of protection by tapping your third eye and visualizing the white light of protection.

3. Squeeze your Power Fist as a trigger and call forth Goddess energy.

4. Carry out your ritual or ceremony, or cast a specific spell, as you desire.

If you have lots of time, or if the magick you need to perform is serious and important, it is always good to do a full ceremony for best results. Add these steps to the previous ones as you did in your Self-Initiation: cast your Circle; call on the Watchtowers to lend their powers; have the Elements present and speak a few words to each in appreciation; call on your guides, ancestors, or beloved ones to assist you; and always speak directly to the Goddess to make your magick meaningful and effective.

A full ceremony is most effective in healing spells, or in any ceremonies meant to help, assist, relieve, lend comfort to or heal the mind, body, or soul. I have a friend, Eroca, who is an excellent healer. She says to imagine the healing qualities of a light that is dark blue-violet in color, filling up the ailing part of the person being healed. I'd follow that advice, because she works wondrous healing magick.

This much is true, my initiate: When you work your deep magick on behalf of the Forces of Good, you simply can't go wrong. However, if you do anything negative or hurtful, your energy is guaranteed to boomerang—it will come back three times as harmful as what you sent out. Yikes! That is the universal law of weaving magick. It is the responsibility of all powerful women to use their gifts of magick only to better the world. I have faith in your good judgment and caring nature. You have strongly pledged to work on behalf of the Forces of Good, and that has been registered and can't be undone.

Maintain the deep and abiding faith in yourself and the Goddess, you hardworking spiritual seeker, and watch with true delight as your newfound abilities and personal magick bring enchantment to your life.

Goddess School Spells That Really Work

Where and when do you use your magick? It doesn't have to be a heavy, serious matter each and every time. I've used my magick to influence exam results. Sure, I studied hard, but the butterflies in my stomach almost paralyzed me when I actually sat down to write the exam.

School exam charm

In high school, I wrote a spell to relax me and to open the energy waves in my mind. So can you. Once everyone else in the class had their test paper and bent their heads to begin working furiously, here's what I did: I would pause, press my pen or pencil to my forehead, take three deep breaths, quickly cast my Lorica, and relax with a quiet sigh.

Then I'd close my eyes for concentration and whisper the invocation I had prepared in advance. I asked that all I had studied would return clearly to my relaxed mind; that I'd express myself clearly and correctly; and that I'd manage my time well so that I finished every question (a big problem I had until my spell). Finally, I'd open my test and begin to do it with the renewed faith and relaxed confidence that the Goddess was standing beside me. And She always was. So I believed; so it happened.

Public speaking spell

Honestly, is there anything we fear more? Public speaking is the stuff of nightmares. In fact, I read that more adults have re-occurring dreams about standing in front of class to speak in all kinds of embarrassing situations, such as wearing their slippers or pajamas and, yes, even standing there naked!

This strong spell requires advance preparation. The problem is not researching and writing your speech—the Goddess will help you—it's the 40 faces staring straight at you that gives you the willies. You need a positive spell with a trigger to use when you actually have to (gulp) stand up there at the front of the class, open your mouth, and hope something intelligible comes out. A *really* effective spell would make them all go away for the 10 minutes you have to speak!

When preparing the spell, see yourself standing there speaking. Imagine the audience is only your mother smiling at you, or maybe it is your very dearest and most trusted buddy. See them listening intently to your speech. Experience that relaxed feeling of being with them and no one else. You can do no wrong. Once you've got that safe and comfortable feeling, cross the fingers on your right hand to lock it in. Then write a positive chant that you can repeat on your way to school.

Just before you get up to speak, take three deep breaths, cross your fingers and let that feeling of comfort and safety flow through you as you walk to the front of the class. During the speech, don't look directly at anyone. Simply move your eyes, back and forth across the audience, and deliver that killer speech to your mom or your best friend. Watch them smile and applaud. It worked for me.

Custom design a bunch of school spells

You know best what bugs you about school, what terrifies you the way public speaking did me. Decide that your magick can solve these problems. Realize it can disarm bullies, neutralize nasty situations, and even silence spiteful gossips when you or a friend are concerned.

Plan your spell; prepare carefully; believe in the goodness and rightness of what you are doing; harm no one in your effort; remember to include a physical trigger to summon all the good energy; and write a neat little chant and repeat it, over and over. Now that's what effective spells are all about.

chapter 16

Look Up, Way Up! Moon Magick

There is a strong influence in your Maiden Magick life that you may be overlooking, an important element that will play a large role in your spiritual life.

What is it?

The moon. It is the strong influence of Mother Moon above you each and every night. In urban, suburban, and even much of today's country living, the moon doesn't recieve a second thought. And what a mistake! What a great teacher you are passing by.

The ancients valued the moon and understood the magick it holds, because they were outside so much of the time with just a tiny campfire, a smoky torch, or, perhaps later, a dim lantern. The sky, before electricity created a haze of dull pale light, was unbelievably bright. The stars were clear, ever twinkling, and easy to distinguish. But it was the moon that cast the only real night light that mattered. And to the tribespeople, she smiled down and had lots to tell them.

They could forecast coming weather by nightly changes in the moon's size and appearance. The diviners noted her shape, and the light or clouds surrounding her, to forecast good or bad fortune coming to the tribe. The magick of her gravitational pull influenced the tides as well as the menstrual cycles of all women's bodies, and the ebb and flow of their sexual rhythms. She was more than worthy of close study and high respect.

But what about the sun?

Ah yes, the world is full of sun worshippers these days, isn't it? Many early faiths around the world put great stock in the importance of the sun, and some thought he was a god. But to the Clan Mothers, he was no big deal. Frankly, the brash old sun was "boring" and irrelevant when it came to their rituals, ceremonies, and forecasts of the future. You see the sun, bright as it is, just goes from East to West each day with the same predictable results. Mister sun gives light and warmth, but no real magick. The Goddess Sulis, who is associated with the town of Bath in England, was said to use the heat of the sun for healing, but that's about it. With the exception of the occasional sunset that could knock your socks off, the sun did little to contribute to the mysteries of life because he simply never changed.

But Mother Moon, as the Celts called her, changed every single night. She became their calendar and their master of the tides. And under the pull of the moon's full face, even more newborn babies than usual were pulled kicking and screaming into Abred. Pregnant mothers, heavy with child and ready for birth, were always glad to see the full moon coming around to help bring their baby forth. She seldom let them down. Even today, hospitals often put extra nursing staff in the maternity rooms during the full moon.

And when a maiden was blessed with her first menstrual cycle—yes, you heard me right—coming into womanhood was considered a time for joyous celebration. The first menses of a maiden was genuine evidence of the Goddess dwelling within her, for menstrual blood was associated with fertility and considered sacred. You are aware that the cycles of Mother Moon—28 days—echo your own menstrual cycle. Many Witch covens don't like to go longer than 28 days between the celebration of festivals or Sabbats honoring the Goddess.

The Moon's progress across the sky was the ultimate proof of the revolving cycles of life. She would change nightly, a dependable cycle that moved slowly from utter darkness to the bright light of the full moon and back to the dark. The people saw her change, watched her waxing and waning. She was the ultimate example of the Goddess' birth/death/regeneration cycle that touches all our lives. The moon was a presence. The same holds true today.

Start by looking up. She is still there, waiting. She still watches over you and She is happy for you to learn the meaning of her many changing faces, her many moods. Take some action at the next full moon (check your regular calendar for the pictures of the moon phases beside the numbers). Then, on the night of the full moon, turn off the TV or shut off the computer. Go outside and bathe in spectacular silvery moonlight, or go ahead and dance under her smiling face. It will make you feel yummy inside.

But to really celebrate her, go ahead and arrange a Moon Magick party with your girlfriends. It will be a blast. It will celebrate the changing cycles on your Goddess Path and reenforce your commitment to sisterhood. I'll help you plan it.

Moon Madness

Here are some fun things to learn about
Celtic traditions regarding changes in the face of Mother
Moon. Remember this terminology: The waxing moon means it
is getting bigger; while the waning moon gets smaller, going from
a full moon back down to nothing or the dark of the moon.

New Moon   Means new beginnings. A good time for a formal
healing spell to be cast, for positive results are
assured. An excellent time for blessing new ven-
tures, new relationships, new babies, or coming
travel. The Celts believed that whatever weather
accompanied the New Moon, that same weather
would last all 28 days.

Half Moon   The Druid Moon. They believed the Moon-Between-
the-Halves was fortunate, and that light was
especially bright on the sixth night of the waxing moon, making this a most sacred time. Use
this time for spells that need a surge of moon
energy: healing for someone who has been de-
pressed; or for positive changes to something
that has been worrisome in the past.

Full Moon   A time of celebration. For maximum light, maximum gravitational pull, and most awesome pres-
ence, the full moon can't be topped. A face can
be detected in the full Mother Moon; as a child,
I always thought She was puckering her lips and
saying, "Oh, my." Many dances, rituals and hon-
ors are paid to Her under Her full visage.

Dark of Moon The time when no moon appears or does or doesn't seem to. The Goddess is in the Otherworld. Lay low. Don't start anything new. Use the time to reflect, re-consider, relax.

Obscured When the face of Mother Moon was covered by clouds, or misted over with a hazy light, the diviners were called in to decide what that meant to the Clan. Normally a cloud-covered full moon meant trouble was brewing, and the halo around the moon was called "greasy." It meant rain or dangerous storms coming.

Waxing Moon Because this is the time when the moon is going from new to full and growing brighter, it is a good time for any rituals or ceremonies where you want a spell that needs the energy of growth and expansion and fullness—such as the desire for a relationship to grow, a child's health to improve, or a project to be completed successfully.

Waning Moon The time of the full moon is passing and Her glow diminishes. This is still a good time for spells that relate to a quieting down, a turning off of the attention or energy. For example, after a scandal, or some other wild and negative time, a person might want a little peace and calm. This is the perfect time to conjure the energy of serenity. It is also a great time to draw the strength of harmony for anyone.

Love Moons The Celts believed that when a maiden first glanced at a new moon, she could make a love wish. If you turn away from the new moon and it appears over your left shoulder, the time is unlucky for love that night; over the right shoulder means it is fortunate for love that night; and if it straight behind it means you will enjoy good luck all month long.

Celtic Moon Names

There are 13 months in the Celtic calendar named for 13 different trees. Each month (from moon) was 28 days, plus the extra day left over that was set aside for the dead at Samhain on October 31. The 13 moons had their own names as well, based on the work to be done that month, or the particular homage due to the Goddess.

The Blood Moon, for example, is an ancient name that indicated the time when farm animals were slaughtered if there wasn't enough grain to get them all through the long Winters. Later, the Danish Vikings taught the Celts how to grow and keep forage for the animals and the Blood Moon became largely symbolic. The Mead Moon was the month when the honey was gathered and the golden mead wine was prepared and set to barrels. The Oak Moon, at the darkest time of the year, reminded the tribes of the hope and spiritual renewal signified by the Oak tree. It is neat to be able to recognize and call your Mother Moon by her proper name, because it connects you to that spiritual time:

Month	Moon	Month	Moon
November	Snow Moon	May	Dvad Moon
December	Oak Moon	June	Mead Moon
Early January	Wolf Moon	July	Wort Moon (the base of Ale)
Late January	Storm Moon		
February	Chaste Moon	August	Barley Moon
March	Seed Moon	September	Wine Moon
April	Hare Moon	October	Blood Moon

Awesome Fact
Looking for Love? Moon Craziness

Here's a bit of a loony lover's superstition from ancient times that you'll probably want to take a pass on. You need a dark night when the new moon is clear to carry it out—and a trans-Atlantic flight.

Some believed that when a maiden sees a new moon in the new year (night of October 31) she should take her stocking off one foot and run with one foot bare, over the meadows to the next stile. (Yikes! It's almost Winter!) A stile is the stairway built against the stacked stone fences you see in England and Ireland. Stiles were there so that people could cross to the next farm, but the cattle couldn't.

Once the maiden was at the top of the cold stairs of the stile, she must look between her bare big toe and the next toe, and there she should find a hair that will be the color of her unknown future husband's hair. Then she had to walk home backwards and speak to no one the rest of the night.

Walking backwards, one bare foot, and it's almost November—who could be that desperate? And what is hair doing up on top of the stone fence? Oh, and what color are the cattle in the field? Might that be a factor here? Anyway, I hope the wee maid didn't come down with pneumonia and miss her wedding altogether.

Let's pass on that one. Agreed?

Plan a Moon Magick Party

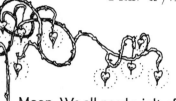

Get together some kindred spirits who are willing to try something new (guys can come, too) and throw a party to Toast the New Moon. We all need a jolt of "new beginnings" energy to carry us forward, so here's a bit of planning to help stage a knock-out party.

Invitations

The crescent Moon is easy to draw and cut out, so it's a natural for the invitations. Ask everyone to: (a) bring an open and positive attitude; (b) bring something to drink; and (c) to wear something white (black dress is for the full moon ceremonies). Tell them when and where the party begins. Most moons are fully visible by 11 at night even in the summer, but make it earlier if you wish.

You Bring

- ◎ A big earthenware bowl (pottery), preferably dark or black.
- ◎ A jug full of water to fill it.
- ◎ A water-based magick marker to draw the moon on the back of your guests' left hands.
- ◎ Music: Find all the great songs you can with "Moon" in them, then burn a CD.
- ◎ Bake or buy cookies shaped like crescent moons.
- ◎ Make up or bring bottles of some sparkling drink that's white (or clear).
- ◎ Be creative, make anything moon-related, or moon shaped, for the favors or food.

What to do at the ceremony

Goddess parties always included some serious spiritual reflection or ritual before the fun could begin. First, you must decide how much ritual to do with these friends. You may want to cast the Circle around everyone, and you may have the representatives of the Elements there, and you may welcome the Watchtowers—or not—it is up to you and how you relate to this particular group of friends. Thirteen tea candles set in a circle on the grass is very attractive, and not too scary for first-timers.

When you have done all you think appropriate for this gathering, and I trust your judgment on this, add these "new moon ritual" steps. Don't forget, you can create your own words, but here is an example:

New Moon Ritual

Gather in a circle inside the ring of candles, with the bowl of water in the middle, and hold hands. The water reflects the new moon and marks its movement, symbolically melding the two planes of Earth and the heavens. If you can place it so that all can see the moon's reflection on the surface of the water, all the better, but that is a bit hard to do.

What you say and do

Start by casting your Lorica around yourself and all your friends.

Only you say:

> **Great Mother, Bless our ritual**
> **Forgive any mistakes**
> **Our hearts are full of pure intent**
> **Harm be to no one**

You raise your arms open to the starry sky and say in a clear, loud voice:

Mother Moon in the blush of your new face
Grant us the gift of your new moon glow
Bless this time, bless this place
May our fortune grow
And good luck flow.

Then you say, and they repeat after you, line by line:

Mother Moon
Fill our hearts with new moon light
Fill our minds with new moon light
Fill our souls with new moon light
Bless our days with fortune bright.

With your Moon
May our fortune grow
And good luck flow.

Blessed by Three
Blessed Be.

Bid the Watchtowers farewell if they were included, and close the Circle.

Cakes and wine party time

Play the CDs. Eat the food. Drink the beverage. Splash your faces with Moon Water from the bowl. Dance. Worship the Goddess on the silken wings of your young laughter.

Part Five

Have No Fear—
You Are Never Alone

CHAPTER 17

The Thrill of Oneness—Your Ecological Self

Do you care about the Earth, about the protection of endangered species, about clean air and sweet water? I bet you do. Well, surprise! You are right on track because concern about our environment is the basic code of the Clan Mothers' teachings. The Earth is the physical manifestation of the Mother Goddess and to honor Her is to dedicate your efforts to preserving the world She gave us. To be one with nature is to be one with the Goddess.

There are many Witches today who follow the Green Way, or declare themselves Green. They adore nature, worship there, and weave their Earth-healing Magick with the aid of herbs. To believe in the Goddess is to extend that belief to caring for Her planet so, in truth, everyone who walks the Goddess Path is inherently Green. And Kermit the Frog sang, "It's not easy being green."

Hey! You already know that. To stand up and speak out about the environment is to be unpopular and out of sync with the corporate-profit mindset of the material world. I never believed the two cancelled each other out entirely, for there are many responsible corporations who have successfully blended their fine stewardship of the environment, and concern for their employees' health and welfare, with strong profit margins. Granted it takes more effort, but it has been done and I applaud each and every one of them.

What can you do? More than you can imagine. Start small, educate yourself, read more, learn more, get yourself a pet if you don't have one, because those adoring animals happily and naturally extend and enhance your sensitivity for all that is living in Abred. Check out groups at school who meet and contemplate what they can do effectively, and where they can best put their efforts to protect the environment. You'll have the added bonus of meeting plenty of like-minded friends in the ecology groups and you'll learn so much along the way.

Your Clan Mothers saw the planet as the body of the Goddess. Its mountains and rolling hills were her curves and muscles; its oceans, lakes, rivers, and streams were her precious fluids. She was everywhere, and in everything. How can we separate our love of nature from ourselves? We are One. Once the world was pristine and healthy. With your help, Abred will be that way again.

Mother and I Are One

Years ago, I read a very interesting book on new scientific discoveries that gave an account of an experiment in subliminal messaging. Subliminal messaging means sending out information that the eyes, ears, or senses can't take in, but the subconscious can—or so the scientists believe. In this particular trial, held in the research labs of an eastern university, student volunteers were given a number of different subliminal messages as the researchers struggled to find the right message that would result in stimulating them to improve their marks at school.

The many one-line messages they tried had mixed or very disappointing results. The researchers were at the end of their rope when someone suggested the line, "Mother and I are One." The author didn't report who suggested this line, or why. In any case, they tried it on one group. Every morning for a period of time the students in the trial would go to the lab and listen to rock music. Subliminally embedded in the music was the line, "Mother and I are One."

The results with those students were astounding. Not only did their marks soar, but their lives dramatically improved. These students reported to the researchers that a number of difficult or insurmountable problems in their lives were solved, relationships improved, and their overall happiness levels and sense of well being went sky high.

It was amusing to read how the scientists tried feebly to explain the link, and even admitted they didn't understand why this message worked so well. But, hey, it was clear to me. Is it to you? Subliminally, the scientists had reached the Goddess within each student and, naturally, She responded to their every need.

But you don't need a special subliminal messaging machine. Just say it to yourself every morning, before you write a test, or meet a loved one, or face a challenge. Go for it. **Mother and I are One.** Could anything be more simple—or effective? No way.

Feeling low? Here's a quick pick-me-up chant:

> **Goddess with me**
>
> **Goddess of me**
>
> **Goddess in me**
>
> **Mother and I are One.**

CHAPTER 18

Hello Grandma, Is That Really You?

There is a comforting truth in following the Goddess Path: Clan Mothers taught young women that they never walk alone. There are spirits and helpmates from beyond with you all the time, watching over you, giving a hand, and assisting you along the bumpy parts of your life journey. What a yummy thought.

Could it be that your beloved grandma, or another grandparent who passed over to Avalon, is still around you? Is she there when you need her? Can you call to her, talk with her? Here's the most excellent news—darn right! Your ancestors in the spirit world guide and assist you each and every day. It has always been that way, and always will be. Now that you are an initiate on your Goddess Path, you are able to communicate with the spirits who are assigned to help you.

I know this for a fact because I was raised communing with the spirits. My own dear grandmother, called Nannie, died before I was born; yet, she was a strong influence in my life from the other side. My mother taught me that women, and loving men, who pass into Avalon have the right to linger here, to stay around to love and guide their children and their grandchildren. In some cases, that may extend another generation, if need be. So if you sometimes feel the presence of a beloved relative who has crossed over, or you feel you need their love and guidance—there is fabulous news for you—they are by your elbow, or at your beck and call, and they watch over you all the time.

Although I referred to your grandma, who may or may not be alive and kicking, what I really mean is that you have a spirit or guiding force of goodness who is watching over you. They are there for you in difficult emotional times, and they are devoted to your well being and care. We are surrounded by numinous helpers from the spirit side.

To the Clan Mothers, it was often the faeries and the brownies who inhabited the other side of the veil, and lived with and beside them in their cottages. My own mother always had a brownie she'd talk to in the house. He was known to be full of mischief and could have her laughing out loud when something she was sure she'd put safely away was found in a crazy, comical place instead. She recognized the work of her house brownie and chided him while she chuckled. I have a high-back chair in my home for my own brownie to sit in and watch over us. And when we pack up and move—so does he.

Your spiritual guide is a reassuring presence that has your very best interests in mind at all times. You've sometimes felt their presence; felt that reassuring feeling that they were sitting with you, haven't you? Well, you were correct. If you thought they were near; they were. That is a fact.

Even as children, many people have special invisible playmates with names and identities. Did you? So were those little friends really there? Of course they were. The active imagination, recognizing your need for a loyal friend of your very own, set about to create one, or beamed out a request that was filled by the willingly band of spirits who surround you.

To be with the spirit of someone you loved, or in the company of another loving spirit guide or guardian, is truly an ancient gift from the Goddess. Lucky you. You need never be lonely again.

How to Recognize Loving Spirits

"Auntie, how do I know if it really is my grandma?"

When a spirit comes to visit, it brings a natural feeling of serenity, for they enter your plane with ease and gentleness. Often they will appear in dreams and that is really a visitation, rather than a run-of-the-mill dream.

If you think you feel your grandma's presence, or if you call her to you, then you will experience one of two things that indicate it is her loving spirit:

a. First, you will feel uplifted and a little in awe;

b. Or you will experience the same warm, special feeling of relating to her that you shared with no one else.

Maybe you can't recall those special feelings until you actually feel them again in her spirit presence. That is the best indicator. And other things will be familiar, maybe you'll want to launch into a conversation or tell her all about a family member. Is she receptive? Does she wants to hear all about it? That's another clue.

But mostly, you have to trust your maiden intuition. If it tells you this is not your grandma—that it's some mischievous spirit playing with you—then simply tell the spirit it is not wanted and to go away. It will. You are in control. Now and always.

Later, I'll tell you more about how to master the dark side, so you can be full of Goddess confidence when you use your magick to conjure up the sprit of someone you love. But hear me clearly: in all likelihood your grandma did respond to your request for a visit. She'll be as pleased as you to communicate.

ENJOY YOUR TIME TOGETHER.

chapter 19

Grandma, I Need Your Help

Now that you know your grandmother (or another loving ancestor or spirit guide) is there, how can you talk with her, or learn from her special brand of knowing wisdom?

Learning to talk with the spirits is a surefire way to enhance the quality of your life, your confidence, and your magick. When you follow the steps outlined later for communicating with (or channeling) your ancestors, you will feel a definite broadening of your spiritual awareness, and you'll soon begin to trust your intuition and decisions more readily. By exercising your spirit connections, and your channeling muscles, you'll put a shine on your spiritual self-esteem. You will feel more relaxed, and you'll find a fresh appreciation for nature and for all the great people in your life. That's a terrific head space to be in, isn't it?

When talking with your grandma or spirit guides, I've always found it is best *not* to ask direct questions, or questions that require a yes or no answer. Don't ask the spirits to make decisions on things such as: *Should I date Jeremy?* or *Should I go to a high school closer to my house?* Frankly, these are your decisions; the spirits have better things to do, and a lot more to show you if you are open to it.

But I need to know. What should I say, then?

Talk it all out with them. Discuss this potential boyfriend. Tell them all about him and weigh the pros or cons of his personality, his attitude, and about getting involved with him, or not. How do you talk to the spirits? Speak in your thoughts as though you were having a conversation; or go ahead and talk out loud if you are walking along, or at your outdoor altar, for example. Say your side and "hear" the answer in your thoughts.

And on that question about the high school choice? Talk about everything involved with that decision as well. Like, what you think you'll enjoy about going there or what you may not like about going there. Simply keep the question *Should I/ Shouldn't I?* in the back of your mind. After a few days, you'll notice that the answer is amazingly clear to you. You'll find your thoughts say, *"Date Jeremy? Over my dead body! What was I thinking?"* Or about that new school? Maybe your thoughts are favoring the move: *"Yep, it'll be more convenient, not as much travel, and I'll meet new friends in my own neighborhood. Hmm, I have a good feeling about it."* You have your answers and they both feel right. The spirits helped you sort it out.

This is a bit of a surprise when talking with spirits: much of the conversation goes on in your own mind. At first, you don't know whether to trust this—are you just making it up, or what? But after awhile, you will sense the difference because there is a real conversation of give and take going on. Some of the ideas your grandma introduces—well, you wouldn't have dreamed them up yourself, so they are clearly coming from beyond. Trust the process, and you'll soon know by the results that you were really hearing what they had to say to you.

Okay. Ready to pick up the great cellphone in the sky? Follow the steps outlined here and connect!

How to Communicate With Your Ancestors and Spirit Guides

" Aunt C.C., I think I'm ready to talk to my grandma. Where do I start?"

Important question, my spiritual seeker, for I know you want to do it right, don't you? The answer is much simpler that you could ever imagine. The plain truth is that when you think about a loved one on the other side—and we'll use grandma as an example again—she *is* there. Presto! Without hesitation, her spirit arrives to be with you.

Telepathy, channeling, or the calling up of spirits has instantaneous results. Trust me on that. No waiting. No delays. You simply have to summon up her memory, to think about her in your mind, and she is there. Awesome!

It is a bit of a magick trick, isn't it? Think of all the loving spirits manifest right near you who are always ready to listen, or lend a hand, or aid you in some way. Wish for them, and your wish is always granted. Now that is very reassuring, isn't it?

Here are the steps for communicating with that terrific spirit guide assigned to you or with your own one-in-a-million grandma.

1. Sit in a quiet place (bright or sunny is best). Always cast your Lorica. As with all communication with the otherside, caution is the best way to go. Take your three cleansing breaths. Opening yourself to channeling is an easy process, even easier than meditation. And don't forget you are always in control. If you don't like what is happening—stop it with Goddess confidence. I'll tell you how in the next chapter, so be sure to read on. There are certain cautions to be observed, and tricks for controlling your communications with the Otherworld. Read it, too, before you actually try to channel.

2. It is important to focus your mind. That is, picture your grandma as you knew her at her best, or from a photo of her that you love. Ask the Goddess and all the Forces of Good to be with you, to help you. Take a moment to relax your body and to raise your thoughts to the heavens. Concentrate your mind on her visit and don't let your thoughts stray. If they do, drag them back to the task. Bring relaxed peace into your mind.

3. Then ask in your mind, or say: *"Grandma (or my spirit guide), please come to me."* Now, know in your heart that she is standing by you. Greet her and blow her a kiss if that would be natural. Tell her you love her. Thank her for coming and notice the joy you feel, or any other impressions or sensations that you recognize as familiar, comforting and related to your Grandma as you knew her.

4. Talk with her in your mind or aloud. Tell her all your troubles, if you need to. Pour them out. She is there to listen and to help you. Ask for her advice and be aware of what comes immediately to mind in response to your question.

Here's an example: Maybe you are driven half-mad by your bossy sister, and you tell Grandma so. She may tell you, in your thoughts, that your sister has a lot of problems or challenges that you don't have; and that you need to love and forgive her when, in fact, you don't feel that way at all toward your sister right now. But it's your goodly Grandma speaking, isn't it? Maybe it's good advice. And hearing that your sister has some problems—well, it kind of makes you warm up to her a bit, doesn't it? Then maybe it occurs to you that you haven't done any fun things with your sister for a while, as you used to do, and that maybe you should set up an outing for just the two of you. Hey, is your grandma smiling at you?

Go ahead, visit with your grandma all you want. And when you are finished your visit, ask her to come again. Then bid her farewell and thank her for her heavenly visit.

Now read the following chapter *before* you begin.

chapter 20

Become a Master of the Dark Side

Here's a truth about the Otherworld: There are some spirits, undeveloped entities, who act as tricksters or simply like to bug you—but you hold the key to banishing them in an instant. You need to learn to recognize them when they muscle their way into your visits with kindly spirits; and, with the help of the Goddess, you will learn to show them the door as quickly as they came bursting in.

The most important thing to know in case one of those lower-level spirits sneaks in is that you are in complete control. You have the power to send him packing. Without a doubt. Believe it and be confident, so that mixed up or negative messages don't come to you from the Otherworld. Protecting yourself with your Lorica is absolutely essential before you visit with the spirits. Pledge to always cast that light of protection.

When you channel your grandma, for example, there may be times when you feel something is amiss, that your grandma would "never say that!" That's a clear sign that the tricksters are playing with you. Or if the advice is negative or nasty, you can sense their presence. You have to stop what you are doing and call on the Goddess, for She'll gladly intervene. Read and heed the warnings that follow.

The important thing is to proceed with Goddess confidence. You are an accomplished spiritual seeker with a magickal kit bag of your own creation, so you are no pushover when it comes to spiritual matters. But as with everything else worth doing, and doing well, you need to study the steps to avoid psychic dangers.

Warning! Avoid Psychic Dangers in Channeling

You are channeling your grandma but something is wrong, something is seriously out of whack, and you don't want to go a step further in that game. Your Grandma comes from a high vibration of love. Spirit guides are also evolved to a high and clear vibration of goodness and love. Accept no substitute.

So if something about your grandma doesn't feel right—if she doesn't seem like your grandma—call on the Goddess immediately. **SOS.** Ask Her please to lead this spirit away to a higher place. Say to the trickster:

Go in peace, leave me!

There you did it! The lower entity is gone. Vanished. And the Goddess won't let it back.

So, have you lost your spiritual connection to your Grandma? Nope. Not at all. Simply wait just a moment, relax, picture your Lorica, then call your grandma again and ask the Goddess and all the heavenly spirits who guide you to bring her to you now. She'll be there. Feels like her now, doesn't it? Good. Go on with your great visit.

In the unlikely event you again hear negative advice from your grandma, or anything contrary to her kindly nature—**end the session immediately!** It may be that other wily lower entities are still trying to crash your party. Once again, ask the Goddess to whisk the mischievous spirits away and command them to:"*Go in peace, but go now.*"

Then relax and take a break from channeling for a few days.

I like to think of it this way: Sometimes there are days when static interference from the cosmos plays havoc with radio and satellite transmissions here on Abred. Maybe the spirit world is like that too. Remember: True spiritual guidance is always positive and loving because it is channeled from the Forces of Good. Never settle for less.

Become a Psychic Bouncer

Now you've got the dirt—the dark side can try to come around and hassle you sometimes. But just living life every day, you've had a taste of the dark side of Abred, haven't you? Makes Goddess sense that there would be a flip side to the Otherworld, too.

So how do you use your magick to counteract that dark side and keep the light glowing white in your life? Here are some more tips for getting rid of unwanted spirits, entities, or paralyzing fears once and for all:

1. Whenever you have a scary nightmare that wakes you up in a sweat, all shivery and shaky, sit up and call on the Goddess to take those horrid visions away. Cast your Lorica, make a Power Fist with your left hand, take the index finger of your right hand and trace the outline of a capital "G" on your forehead. You'll sleep in peace now. But in the safety of the morning, ask yourself what those warnings in your dreams meant. Try to relate the scary parts to some stress or fear you have in your waking hours, and make an effort to resolve them.

2. Sometimes you are awake and frightened for some reason. Maybe you are overloaded, or over tired, and you feel very anxious. To banish all that negativity, first cast your Lorica, then—sing! Yes, you heard me right. Sing out loud. Hymns? Sure, if you know some. Or repeat the same one over and over. Rock songs? Absolutely. It is the sound of the song that banishes

all the dark and fearful aspects of the Otherworld. I know from experience that they hate the sound of singing even if, unlike me, you happen to sing in key. They still flee.

Maybe you remember hearing an old song from the musical, *The King and I*, that says "just whistle a happy tune" whenever they are afraid. Well, it's great advice. Try it. You'll be delightfully amazed at the good results.

3. You've just lost something really, seriously important. You're late and your ride is waiting outside, beeping the blasted horn. In a panic? It could be tricksters at work driving you half-mad. Your heart is beating hard, you are pulling things out of drawers and turning over piles of papers, throwing clothes and shoes out of the way. Ugh! You know you've been there. Stop!

Sit down. On the floor, the stair, the bed. It's time to call up your magick to neutralize this trickster. Cast your Lorica. Make your Power Fist. Ignore the honking horn. Take three cleansing breaths. Call on the Goddess to help you find the lost article.

Close your eyes and see the article clearly. Is it keys? Speak to them while you get a vivid picture and order them to reveal themselves. See the color of the key chain, the bobbles and dangles that hang on it? The gleam of the metal keys? Now adjust your visualization a bit, like a movie camera panning back slowly. Imagine the context of where the keys are lying. Red plaid like the inside of your jacket pocket in the hall? Blue and fuzzy like the carpet? Where?…under the bed! Bingo. Bango. You see them. You magickal wonder, you, see what you've done? You just out tricked the trickster!

DARKNESS: BE GONE!

Journaling—
My Spiritual Visitation

DATE OF VISIT:

SPIRIT'S NAME:

MESSAGE OR ANSWERS GIVEN:

ACTION TAKEN BY ME:

Add later:

DATE OF JOURNAL ENTRY:

RESULTS OF SPIRITUAL ADVICE TO ME:

Part Six

Work Fun Magick on Yourself, Friends, and Boyfriends

chapter 21

Get Real!—Time to Take the Celtic Long View

The Clan Mothers held great store in having their Initiates learn the shapeshifting skill of the Long View, and applying it to their life decisions. How did the Long View work for the clan, and what does it have to do with the power of your magickal skills or your trip down the Goddess Path?

When the Clan Mothers were worried about the tribe's welfare, or how best to prepare for the coming seasons, they called in their specially trained diviners or fortune tellers to conjure some magickal forecasting. The diviner used the technique known as the Long View to "see," based on where things stood at that moment and projecting forward to arrive at a vision of the future, assuming the tribe went merrily along its way without change. If the Clan Mothers didn't like what the diviner saw, they took positive steps to change that future. Can the future actually be influenced, altered, or redesigned?

Hey! Make note of this all-important truth that the Celts knew so well:

YOU, MY ACCOMPLISHED INITIATE, HAVE THE ABILITY
TO CHANGE THE FUTURE AS IT IS NOW WRITTEN;
YOU CAN MAKE IT BRIGHTER AND BETTER.

So, you wonder, what value was the Long View to the tribe? Well, here's an example: If, in the early Autumn, the diviner wove her spells and saw hunger among the tribe at the end of the long, harsh Winter, the Clan Mothers would know to store more food than planned and to distribute it with measured caution until Spring, so that even if everyone grew thin, widespread hunger would be averted. They would take measures to alter the future to serve their needs and ensure their survival. As the wise ones of the clan, they used the magick of the Long View to save the lives of many people.

Here's another example: If the diviner saw the tribe suffering from a terrible rash and sore, bleeding gums before the Spring light broke through, the healers and herbalists would be summoned to work together to concoct a special tonic that would give the people enough vitamins and healing herbs to prevent that health problem from happening. Thinking ahead through the Long View, and facing the reality of the future as it will unfold if nothing changes, allowed them to change course— to fix things before disaster happened.

So, naturally, as an Initiate, the Aunties would instruct you to apply the Long View to your own life. They'd ask you to weave a little magick on yourself. You would go to a quiet place, see yourself stepping out of your sneakers, and using the magickal art of shapeshifting. Then you'd take a good hard look at the eventuality of your own life, imagining your future. Do it without emotion, the Aunties would caution, so you can realistically evaluate the next 10 or 15 years and see where your current Path will lead you, if you don't make any meaningful changes.

As a young maiden in the clan, they would ask you to consider what your future would hold if you married hastily, without careful thought; or if you ran off and joined another tribe far away. Initiates were to see themselves clearly in all possible and natural developments. Sometime the picture wasn't pretty. Sometimes it was almost hopeless, full of suffering, and doing without. Sometimes it was okay but not really great. But armed with that information from their probable future as seen through the Long View, they were given back the reins of control. The future was their horse to ride, or to be pulled along behind. It was their beautiful choice.

So naturally those young Initiates, much like you, began to look at rearranging and rewriting the picture of their future as they would prefer it to be. They could design it to be as grand or as satisfying as they liked. It was clear to them as it is to you. If you see something in the current natural unfolding of your future that you don't like, change it now, while you still can. You can do anything. You are skilled, capable, gifted, and most of all, you are part divine.

By using the shapeshifting magick in the Long View, you will learn about your own needs, desire, and dreams, and how best to attain personal satisfaction, happiness, and deep fulfillment. Start now to face reality and plan for the best. Thanks be to the visionary gifts of your Clan Mothers.

How to Take the Long View

It's time to step out from among the leafy trees and take a long look at the forest. Time to examine the course and direction of your education, your social life, and your friendships. With the Goddess as your partner, you may want to make some divine changes in your plans.

Step right up and take the reins of the Goddess Epona's magickal white horse. She was the superstar of Celtic Goddesses—strong, capable, and fearless—just like you. By pledging to take control of your future, you will change your attitude, toss out old worries, and step over crippling fears, shyness, or feelings of inadequacy. The Long View will help you listen to the Goddess guidance within your soul, and walk with confidence along your very own magickally crafted adventure.

The Long View is a magickal tool. You are not only the star of your own play, you have the ability be rewrite the script, rearrange the props, and dress yourself in fine costumes. Yes, the Long View can show you harsh realities that may not be easy to face right now, such as a movie you'd rather not see; yet the Long View also holds beautiful promise. You can create a happy ending. You are the star, the writer, the designer, the director, and even the critic in your life. Wow! You're something else!

The Long View has two separate steps. The first one is akin to slapping yourself across the face with a cold fish. You must consider what might be in store if you don't improve your attitude, your education, or your lifestyle. Cold reality. Yuck! But it leads to the second part, which is the fun part.

In step two, you get to dream a beautiful future for yourself. Once you are clear about what you truly want from life, you need only come back to the "here and now" to make the changes and personal decisions that will make it all happen, actually happen. That's a bit of magick, wouldn't you say?

Designing your future can be a blast. Just follow these few magick steps:

1. Do I still have to tell you the first essential step? *"No. Stop C.C....Cast my Lorica of Protection, right?"* Absolutely. Then...*"No, wait."* Take three cleansing breaths... Yep. *"Ah...then I make my Power Fist and invite the Goddess to be with me, right?"* Hey! I love it when I'm no longer needed—that's real success to a teacher. Thanks be for the compliment. Now add these tricks to your kit bag, wise one:

2. You are in a quiet place. Shut off all rambling thoughts and grow quiet and peaceful inside. Take more breaths to relax, if need be. Now experience a simple Celtic form of shapeshifting. As you sit there, imagine yourself getting up—a transparent copy of yourself—and stand next to the seated you. See yourself still sitting there, and smile. But don't forget—you are always in control and you can reverse this feeling in the blink of your eye, if you need to. When you feel ready, the "standing you" will close her eyes and ask to see your future as it will be—how it will unravel if nothing changes in the way you live your life.

Concentrating on current reality is hard, because your imagination will try to keep the truth from you. If you do fantasize something that simply isn't attainable, based on what you are doing right now and the decisions you're making, press on your belly button and say: *"Stop."* Take a breath, rewind your movie, and start where you left off.

Now picture that you are older, about 29 years old. See yourself dressed in certain clothes, living in a certain set of rooms. Is there a partner there? See that person as they pass through the room you are in. Does he or she say anything to you? What is it, and how is it said—kindly, lovingly, harshly, or crudely? Are there children? How many? How young? How do they respond to you? How do you feel about them? Are you working?

If so, watch as you go outside and drive a certain kind of car to a certain place of employment.

Consider how you feel in your heart and soul. Are you happy? Full of hope and promise? Pleased with yourself and your life choices? Yes or no? You don't have to linger there, especially if the answer is no. Time to click off the movie. Softly whisper:

**Thanks be, Goddess, for the gifts
delivered to me through the Long View.**

Step comfortably back into your "seated self" and open your eyes. Whew! What was that like? A bit of a jolt?

3. Spend the next few days or couple of weeks thinking about your Long View and how you'd like to change it, improve it. Think hard about what you'd really like to see, who you'd want to share it with, and especially how you'd prefer to feel as you live your everyday life. Think about all of it. Look at the lives of your family and friends and then consider what you do and don't want in **your** future. Give it plenty of thought.

4. When you think you are ready, repeat all the steps again, but this time see your Long View as you want it to be, with every delicious detail and beautiful emotion. What do you wear now; how do you feel in your heart and soul? Isn't there joy in living with feelings of accomplishment, of following your true path by developing and using your own gifts? And while you are at it, people your future with great souls. Make your partner absolutely lovable; your relationship close and romantic. Why would you settle for less when you are already an independent and self-sufficient woman?

It isn't about money. It isn't about fame. It is the true satisfaction and joy of being everything you are capable of being—that's true Goddess success.

5. The next step is the hard one. Ask this simple Goddess question: What do I to have to change to make my very brightest dreams come true? Huge question, my Initiate. Hard answers. You can change your future for the better. Yep. You are up for it!

chapter 22

Boost Your Popularity—Recreate Clan Sisterhood

Popularity is important to you. It should be. It is the indication that you belong. Yes, you belong to the Goddess Clan, and that is a lovely feeling, but you need friends on the earth plane to hang with, too. The Aunties knew that; they lived it. It is what sisterhood is all about.

The early women in the tribes naturally spent time together and they made fun out of it. They gathered herbs and dried them, mashed and crushed them, then soaked them in water or oil or wine, and they did this laborious work—together. A whole cottage full of women working so hard, and laughing even harder, that the time flew by. They willingly helped each other with the births of their babies, took special care of the elderly women, and, in their spare time, they spun, sewed, studied, and worshipped together. They laughed and teased each other mercilessly, talked about guys incessantly, and they were always planning parties. Fortunately, some good things never change.

Women of the Clan supported each other through illness, through heartbreaks, and through all the trials life dealt them. Sure there was rivalry and jealousy and a few hissing spats between individuals, but the Clan Mothers were quick to remind them of their need for each other, and the necessity to make amends and fix any fractured relationships.

Celtic sisterhood is often associated with spirituality, as well as community. The nine sisters in the myths about the magick Cauldron of Regeneration were said to keep the pot bubbling by the warmth of their breath alone. Other sisterhoods in legend speak of priestesses living on sacred islands for part of the year, conjuring their magick and observing their rituals, and then returning to their families and their Earthly duties.

The sisterhood had great influence when it came to making peace or stopping violence. Over the centuries, various Councils of Women called the Old Sisters were highly regarded for their ability to prevent battles, or for negotiating difficult peace treaties. Their fine work was considered an example of how cooperation among women of the sisterhood could move mountains.

The basic principles of sisterhood were working together, supporting each other, and making short work of any task when sisters were involved. It was about the amazing power found in group effort. Today it means considering the needs of your girlfriends and female relatives. It is a simple matter of being sensitive and watching to see who might be in some kind of trouble; or feeling blue; or maybe in need of a shoulder to cry on, or a good "talking to." It means being a really good, really caring friend.

Here's the hidden bonus in living the Goddess sisterhood way: By being unselfish and genuinely caring about the girls you know, you naturally and effortlessly become popular. Everyone, and I stress *everyone* wants to have a friend like the person you will become. When you live selflessly; when you are truly interested in others and their well being; when you support and care about other people; when you include every- one and put the code of Goddess sisterhood first and fore- most in your social life; then people want you around them. You are a light. A beacon. You are delightful to know.

But you can't fake it. People see through insincerity, don't they? You have to genuinely start to care about other women, your real sisters of the heart, whom you meet along your God- dess Path. Don't overlook anyone, even the most unpopular girl. There is good in everyone, waiting to be coaxed out of hid- ing. Be kind and gracious to everyone, and people will soon seek you out for the warm approval they feel in your company, and you'll have plenty of friends.

The real reward is in opening your heart and soul to let light and love and human compassion shine through. By being there—really there—for your friends, you will discover your own sense of place and community. That is good Goddess work.

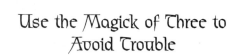

Use the Magick of Three to Avoid Trouble

The Clan Mothers called them the triplicities; the Druids knew them as the Triads. The number three, and its multiples, was sacred to the Celts. Based on the three phases of the Goddess, it was part of the rhythm of their lives and an important element in their legends, poetry, and music. The Druid sages, who were the Celts' philosophers, and great thinkers, organized their lessons into groups of three because they knew the number carried magickal energy.

But as you may suspect, the number has its flip side, too. And nowhere is that clearer than in the chaotic kind of energy that explodes when friendships—important and meaningful friendships—are made up of a cast of three young women. Here, the number three spells disaster to the group endeavor.

Take this fact as a cosmic and practical warning: Even though a friendship of three girlfriends may work at first, the energy force unleashed by the number three must break free in order for each of you to learn, to experience, and to enrich yourselves. Ultimately your cozy little band will break apart. Maybe you've already experienced this force, most women have. It usually ends in hurt and pain as two of the three go off without the other. It can't be helped. It is built into the dynamism of the number three.

Take Auntie C.C.'s advice. If you have a friendship of three that you cherish, have a frank discussion on the force of that number and maybe you can work together to neutralize its dark side. Or, better yet, seriously consider drawing in another friend to experience the unifying energy found in a set of four. Remember the Watchtowers—the cardinal points of North, East, South, and West. Each is independent and distinct, yet all work together in gravitational cooperation and harmony.

Add a fourth friend and watch as any discord you've been experiencing diminishes to a workable level among your group. Four is good. Besides, the more sisters in your circle, the better!

Enjoy the ancient gift of supportive and harmonious sisterhood. It has much to offer all four of you.

Party Time Again! Celebrate Sisterhood at a Sabbat

Hey, you wondrous and fun-crazy Initiate. It's time to start planning another party. We celebrated Mother Moon, and maybe you had a few friends in for Samhain, but twice is not enough. You've been learning more about the Goddess festivals and the Fire holidays, so bring a group of girlfriends together—just sister souls this time—to celebrate another sacred Celtic festival.

Which one? The closest…there's no better excuse for a party. Pick the Sabbat coming up in a few weeks. Study about it; read everything you can. Get together and plan a ceremony in its honor. And remember to keep a sharp Goddess eye out so that you don't overlook any girl who may want to be part of it. No hurt feelings here if you can help it, right? Sisterhood, understanding, and lots of Goddess compassion. That's your Path.

Copy the Celtic way of organizing the bash. Meet several times in advance of the date of the Sabbat. Have some refreshments and work at planning the ritual ceremony together and all the details of the party after, like music and the Cake and Wine part that follows any meaningful ritual.

You've done it before, so you know the drill. You can and do weave Maiden Magick. My, see how accomplished you've become? You know how to write chants and blessings, and you just might compose a special affirmation or two for this ceremony. What do you say? A made-from-scratch festive celebration to enjoy with your sister-friends. Don't forget to give everyone a small task, or a chant or poem to write or just to read. Include and honor everyone present. Plan costumes if you'd like, and choose a safe place where you won't be hassled or teased. You don't want any distractions. Oh…and save a place for your Auntie. I'd love to be there.

chapter 23

Open Your Heart—Celtic Generosity and Hospitality

If you follow the Goddess Path, you must adhere to another code for living that the Celts upheld—sometimes with their very lives. So strong was their belief in lavishing generosity and hospitality on any visitor, friend, or stranger that they'd give up the last of their own food to honor that ancient code of the Goddess.

The Goddess provided the model for the people of the clans. She was generous with her abundance, providing all they needed to survive. She was the goddess of fertility, enriching the land and ensuring the healthy continuation of all living things. Even in the chronicles of the life of St. Brigit, the Irish Christian Saint who was designed to replace the Mother Goddess, Brigit gets into trouble with her family for giving their property and belongings away to those in greater need. This idea of "property redistribution" was central to the clans, as valuable gifts of weapons and jewelry were circulated among families as a symbol of generosity and hospitality.

Auntie C.C., do I have to do that?

Heavens, no! You don't need to go so far as to give your family's property away. But you can consider resurrecting some of the Clan's principles of generous acts, warmth, and hospitality in your own daily life.

And there is something in it for you, too. Just like the caring acts of sisterhood we discussed, the compassion you show through generosity and kindness will draw people to you. In the stressful and often selfish world of teens, you'll be obvious by your generosity and genuine concern for others. It will make you stand out of the crowd. And they'll be shocked out of their boots to discover that you're a heck of a lot of fun as well!

A Spell to Draw Friends

As you proudly walk the Goddess Path, you will follow Her code by doing generous acts and spreading kindness. But in order to enjoy all that Abred has to offer, you need kindred spirits to share your social life. It is all part of the Goddess way—to live a balanced life.

If you feel that your serious spiritual quest is not balanced by a satisfying social life, then create a spell to summon girlfriends—kindred sisters. Fun people with similar interests, but varying talents and gifts, who will make your life vibrant and delightfully unpredictable. Following is a possible spell, or you can compose one from your heart. Be clear in your pure intent and prepare as you have in all the previous spells.

A summoning spell to draw like-minded friends

Goddess Mine
Draw me to sweet laughter
Draw me to light bright
Draw me to true friends
I meet this night

Goddess Mine
Draw me to spirits kindred
Draw me to silly play
Draw me to caring sisters
I meet this day

Sisters bring me kindness
Sisters bring me song
Sisters bring me friendship
Now that I belong.
Blessed be, Goddess mine.

chapter 24

Seeing Boyfriends for Who They Really Are

Before you jump to the Love Spells or practice some Come-to-Me magick, the Clan Mothers want you to consider each guy carefully. Assess them with a clear and critical eye. Make a decision to love or not to love based on the keen animal senses of your heart, mind, and blossoming spiritual intuition. They would recommend a version of the shapeshifting magick of the Long View. Remove yourself from the roller-coaster emotions of the moment. Look long and carefully at who this young man really is, and whether he is right for you. Women can be fierce in their love, so it is best to have a partner worthy of standing up for and protecting on life's perilous journey.

Although the maidens of the Clan enjoyed flirting and partying with the young men of the tribe, the rules were clear. No young woman was to make love before they completed all their levels of training and were fully initiated into the tribe—usually at about 16 years of age. This rule originated out of concern for a maiden's well being, because the midwives knew that the success of a birth was dependent upon a maiden being fully grown and physically strong. They insisted that lovemaking be deferred until then. The young men were committed to this unwritten law and could be held responsible, and even shamed, if it was broken.

The Aunties prepared young women like you in the ways of love, as they did in all life matters. They cautioned them about the traps, dangers, and warning signs to watch for before getting deeply involved with a lad, no matter how good-looking (or "comely" as they said) the lad was. And they used plenty of legends and ancient tales as colorful examples to illustrate their points. One of these teaching tales was called Bluebeard.

Bluebeard was a handsome man who charmed a lovely maiden, swept her away from her family, and took her to live in his grand castle. He treated her well for all she could tell, but he discouraged all visitors, and she soon missed her sisters and her parents. In truth, she was very lonely. Bluebeard had one weird rule: He wouldn't allow her to look in a certain room in the castle.

One fine day, when he was away, the maiden's carefree sisters arrived. They fluttered about the castle, gasping and cooing at all the magnificent rooms and fine furnishings. When they saw the locked door, and learned of Bluebeard's rule, they were wild with curiosity. Finally, they convinced the maiden to open the door and look inside.

Now, I should tell you the Clan Mothers were excellent storytellers. They would describe each scene carefully—who was there and how the room looked. They'd build the suspense in a series of heart-stopping, breath-catching, scream-out-loud moments until...

So, what happened, C.C.?

Oh...right. Well, thank heavens for her sisters' souls, because the forbidden room was a dark dungeon. Deep in that room, far from prying eyes, were the ghastly remains of Bluebeard's many other beautiful wives—he'd killed them all! Yikes! If the maiden's sisters hadn't given her the nerve to stand up for her rights and check out the forbidden room, she'd have been history.

So, what did that legend teach young women of your age? It said to be wary of charm and good looks, if the price is losing your family and your support system, or being slowly and systematically isolated. When we speak of a "Bluebeard" today, it doesn't necessarily mean he'll murder you—it means that he will try to control you, to isolate you, to pull the wool over your eyes, and to suffocate your feisty confidence. So don't fall asleep at the Romance wheel. Keep your soul eyes open.

Warning!
Is He a Bluebeard?
Nine Ways to Find Out

The Clan Mothers' criteria for you to assess the value of a young man and potential lover still work today. Check this out. How does he rate?

	Yes	No	Sometimes
1. Does he speak lovingly of his mother?	☐	☐	☐
2. Does he see the humor in situations?	☐	☐	☐
3. Does he have a temper?	☐	☐	☐
4. Does he display increasing jealousy?	☐	☐	☐
5. Does he treat you with kindness?	☐	☐	☐
6. Does he transform your mistakes into public jokes?	☐	☐	☐
7. Does he usually win and you end up doing what he wants to do?	☐	☐	☐
8. Does he like your girlfriends?	☐	☐	☐
9. Does he respect and support you on your spiritual quest?	☐	☐	☐

Here's how to score:

# 1, 2, 5, 8, and 9.	Score 2 points for Yes 0 points for No 1 point for Sometimes
# 3, 4, 6, and 7.	Score 0 points for Yes 2 points for No 1 point for Sometimes

Total scores:

16–18 points	Grab this guy!
10–15 points	So-so. Keep your feet firmly planted on the ground in this relationship. A Magick Maiden deserves the best.
9 points	Answering "sometimes" to each question will give you 9 points. You don't want a "sometimes" kind of guy.
Under 9 points	Ugh! Run, don't walk, away. You can do much better, my dear heart. You really need to think it through.

chapter 25

You Broke Up!
Healing a Broken Heart

Maybe he was a Bluebeard or maybe you've just outgrown him. Perhaps he was unfaithful or unkind or...whatever. But it's over. Clear and simple. Done. Dead. Kaput.

Yet, there's a lingering problem—you're still obsessed with him. Oh no, you don't necessarily want him back, you just hate to see him with someone else and—drat—you just can't seem to shake the blues. Hey! Don't despair. We've all traveled that shaky walk at one time or another. Maybe you've even been there before.

But now you're on a Path of spiritual discovery and deep women's magick. Dig down into the comfort of your newfound confidence—your magick skills. Let that spiritual growth and the numinous knowledge you've accumulated heal you, make you whole again. The Goddess knows all about relationships and the pain of letting go. Trust Her experience. Trust in those wily Clan Mothers and cast a spell to get over it.

A Spell to Draw Strength and Dispel Heartache

The truth is, heartache can sneak up and sandbag you when you least expect it, such as when you see a former love at a party or hear some juicy tidbit about him and his new love. Ugh! Just when you thought you had a great big lock on your heart, it flies open and spills out. So, for this spell, you need a physical trigger as a reminder that your soul's healing. It's also great for those—"surprise-I-just-bumped-into-him" emergencies.

What is your physical trigger? As you say the following spell (or one you compose yourself), do this: Touch the tip of the baby finger on your right hand to the tip of the index finger on the same hand (it makes a space that sort of resembles an upside-down heart). Press together firmly. Use this trigger whenever you feel emotional upset or heartache coming on, it's something you can do without anyone noticing—even that goofball you used to love.

Healing takes strong Goddess determination. Be very physical in this spell. You are getting rid of the negative energy and drawing positive energy into your heart. Throw open the door and let go of the yucky pain you've been carrying around. Bye-bye.

Repeat the spell three times, imagining the sound of ancient drumbeats: deep, slow, and steady. Each word you speak is a beat on that drum. As you say each word, strike your chest with your left hand in the Power fist, and stamp your left foot to the ground in Goddess resolve, keeping time with

the words. Ha! Look at you. A one-woman-band! No kidding—
you're a mighty woman on a mission, not to be messed with.

Beat, heart, beat.
Goddess, Blessed Be.
Beat, heart, beat.
Set my soul free.

Beat, heart, beat.
Drum my heart calm.
Beat, heart, beat.
Heal me by dawn.

Beat, heart, beat.
Lover, go in peace.
Beat, heart, beat.
All heartache cease.

Beat, heart, beat,
By day's first light.
Beat, heart, beat,
Find me set right.

Beat, heart, beat.
Beat heart, now sweet.

I am free.
Blessed Be.

chapter 26

Drawing Love Energy

My friend Elizabeth always goes straight to the Love Spells first—did you? Ha!

Okay, you have healed from your last relationship. It's in the past and you are stronger for the experience. That is a principle enshrined on your Goddess Path. Every hard knock has built within it a tremendous gift of self-knowledge that brings you closer to your ultimate goal of being true to yourself.

In fact, that last love situation is *so* forgotten that you wonder what you ever saw in him at all. That's a nice feeling. It makes you feel a bit smug for a while. The important thing is that you recovered; you are a strong Goddess.

So what's next? Now you're probably ready to have a new love walk into your life—at least for a while. Want some spell-making help to draw the energy of new love to your life? I'm glad to lend a hand. But first, be clear on the kind of young man you want. Then, simply pull his particular kind of energy to you. What is absolutely crucial is that you do not use names in your spell. Drawing positive energy into your life is a good thing. The Goddess will scout about and find a great candidate worthy of your affection. That's the correct—and only—way to do love spells.

You see, if you name an actual person, your magick could mess with their Zen, so to speak, and that is not a good thing. It could come back on you like a boomerang. You have pledged to use your gift of magick only for the Good. So be it. Name no one in your spell. Think in terms of loving energy sweeping towards you, not a particular person. Keep to the high road and let the Forces of Good bring you armloads of great love-energy along with the right kind of guy for you.

A Spell to Draw Your Ideal Guy

Do all your preparations before you cast this spell. Add to your favorite rock or other talismans something small that is glittery or red, or both. Cut out a heart or have some heart shape represented. Light a red candle.

Summoning Love Spell

By the sound of my laughter,
By the sway of my dance,
Come, fine, sweet love,
Smile at me.

By the glow from my heart,
By the love in my soul,
Come, fine, brave love,
Stand by me.

By the light of Mother Moon,
By the blazing burning sun,
Come, fine, new love,
Be with me.

My hand in yours.
My heart with yours.
My love is yours.
Our dreams entwine.

Come, fine, new love,
Be mine.

Blessed Love,
Blessed Be.

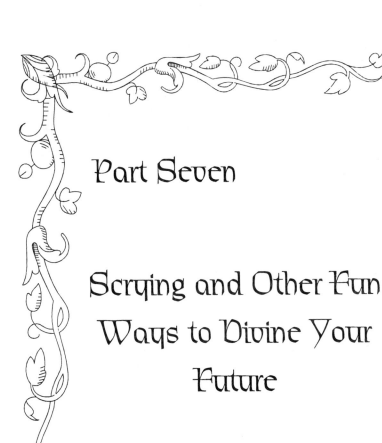

Part Seven

Scrying and Other Fun Ways to Divine Your Future

chapter 27

What the Heck Is Scrying?

Loosen up! Have a blast! Try the Clan Mothers' technique of *scrying,* or fortune-telling.

> *Auntie C.C., what is that?*
> *I don't even know how to pronounce it.*

Scrying is a very ancient way of reading the future to see what lies ahead. It involves foretelling the future by staring into the waters in a cauldron, or dark bowl, with seeds floating on top. It was used to summon up images of things to come. It takes no special equipment or cost outlay, and it's fun. Some people are really good at it. Just bring your magick kit bag, your Lorica, and your terrific sense of fun.

Get a big dark bowl from the kitchen. Fill it almost to the top with pure water (tap water is also fine). Place it on a table in a well-lit room. Put a towel over the bowl while you cast your Lorica, make your Power Fist, and call on the help of the Goddess. Remember, She loves a good time so She'll be delighted to scry with you.

Light a white candle and place it, along with the other representatives of the Elements, near the bowl. Take 13 fennel seeds, or poppy seeds, or any natural seeds from outdoors or your kitchen spice jars and hold them in your left hand. Raise the hand and say:

> **Hear me now!**
> **As my mother's mother's mother**
> **Did before when I was but a dream,**
> **So do I now read the sweet words**
> **Carried on the waters of Her stream.**
> **Clan Mothers show me the way.**
> **Blessed seed,**
> **Blessed by Three,**
> **Blessed Be.**

Remove the towel with great reverence. With the fingertips of your right hand, draw an imaginary line across the bowl, dividing it in half. This is your time measurement. Anything you see in the half of the bowl nearest your body will happen soon. Anything you perceive on the other half will take longer to happen.

Then draw an imaginary line straight down the middle, dividing the bowl in four. This is your directional map. North is the point at the opposite edge of the bowl. West is to the left; East is to the right; and you are seated at the South. Anything you see on the surface may have a directional component, such as: *I see before me a dark-haired man coming from the East* (the right-hand side).

Now say:

> **Great Mother Mine,**
> **Scry me only vivid pictures**
> **From the Bright Side of your Moon.**
> **Scry me joyful, happy scenes**
> **From Your bright Moonbeams.**
> **Blessed Be. Stay by me.**

Now lean over the bowl and cast the seeds gently over the water surface. Ask that the future be revealed for _____ (name a friend who is there or someone you care about). Blow on the seeds and look deep into the water. Squint. Blow on the bobbing seeds a second time, study their movement and then look past them into the water below.

Describe whatever you see in a clear, confident voice as long as your vision is **positive**. If you see something negative, put the towel back over the bowl and ask the Goddess to take the trickster away. Then start again. But with the previous spell words spoken, there is little likelihood that you will be disturbed.

If it is working well, and it is fun to do, then allow people present to ask one clear question each and see if the answer is there. As with all psychic work, stay well in control. If you don't like a question, say so. You run the show. It is important to keep the Forces of Good before you. When you are finished, cover the bowl and thank the Clan Mothers for their assistance. Close your spell with all the appropriate appreciations.

Shake out the towel. Put it on your head and dance around. Then put it on the next person's head and ask them to dance a jig. Continue until everyone does their turn and then break out the refreshments. (I told you it was fun.)

F.A.Q.

But C.C., couldn't I just use a Ouija board?

If this book was online, your speakers would be shaking as I hollered, "**No Way!**" I feel so strongly about this...well, I could just spit.

A Ouija board is a conduit for the lower entities. It's akin to a call to arms for that rabble. They delight in whipping up all kinds of fear and loathing—even pure terror. That really gets them rolling in the aisles with laughter.

The Ouija board is considered an entertainment game by the uninitiated. Nobody ever casts any protection, or calls on the Forces of Good, or exercises any common sense whatsoever. So what do you have? A room full of scared and jittery people moving that little pointer around. Welcome to the monsters' ball.

Here's the absolute truth: I've seen plenty of trickery, confusion, and chaos caused by Ouija boards. All kinds of negative, even destructive, things have come from playing with this "cosmic fire." I heartily recommend that you excuse yourself if one of these toys ever comes out for play.

Don't forget, my initiate, your magick comes from the depths of your being, from your soul. It isn't trivial. It should not be on exhibition in questionable circumstances, or when you are not in control.

JUST SAY NO TO OUIJA BOARDS.

chapter 28

Discover Your future—Clan Style

What are you going to do when you grow up? What job will you have? What work will you do? Will you be suited to it, and it to you?

In the Goddess clans, the Celtic Clan Mothers watched young girls, just like you, to determine the extent of their particular gifts, strengths, or talents. Then they would try to encourage the girls to turn their unique gifts into an occupation that would contribute to the betterment of the tribe. The Clan Mothers might even design a special course of training to help them along.

But training was much different at that time. You didn't go to a big impersonal school; training was often one-on-one—it was more personal and intense. It might mean going to the home of a master of the profession you wanted to learn. For years you would live and learn under that roof. The master craftsperson or professional would treat you with all the affection and respect of a family member, although you'd still be in close touch with your own family. Once you finished your long course as an apprentice, you became a Journey-woman still perfecting your skill for a number of years. Finally, you became a full master. Then the Goddess cycle began anew for, as a master, you were expected to pass your skills along to someone younger and eager to learn.

The Clan Mothers were clever about matching the right trade or profession to the young person. They realized that when you do something you love, you excel at it. You do the job well and with great care, gaining personal fulfillment and satisfaction along the way. A happy worker and a job well done. That's called a win-win situation today.

Well, guess what? That careful assessment of your talents, your special skills, is still happening today. But it's more informal. Your clan elders (your family, close friends, or favorite teachers) have been watching you for years, some with that same eagle eye of the Clan Mothers. What kind of job or profession should you go into? They've got their own ideas about that. Through the years and the many phases of your life, they've noticed where you find your greatest joy, what you are best at, and what comes naturally to you.

If you are at a loss as to what should be your job someday, or if you don't know what training or education you should pursue, then do your own little Clan research. Talk to the friends and family who have known you for a long time, or to the teachers who have taken an interest in you. Ask them what they've noticed. Find out if they have some great ideas about what your career path should be, and how your training and education should be designed. You'll be surprised by what they say. Just ask them.

Okay. It's not cool. The trouble is, young people seldom ask members of their Clan or their extended family for opinions anymore. But you can change all that. Go back to the Goddess Way. Go ahead, ask them what they think you would be happiest doing in life. You've got nothing to lose. At the very least, they'll be flattered you asked. And it *could* be a hoot!

Gathering Up the Clues to Your Future

Here is a revealing personal research project that may have you looking at employment and career opportunities you never considered. Just fill out the form and make up more if there are lots of people to interview. Look at your collected forms and compile the information. It may surprise and delight you.

Ask them these questions and write in the answers:

NAME:

HOW MANY YEARS HAVE YOU KNOWN ME?

WHAT SORT OF THINGS INTRIGUED ME WHEN I WAS LITTLE?
(FOR EXAMPLE, MOTORCYCLES, FASHION SHOWS, PUPPIES, GARDENING, CAMPING, HAMMERING, ETC.)

WHAT PROJECTS DO YOU THINK I'VE SHOWN THE MOST INTEREST IN?
(FOR EXAMPLE, SHOWS ABOUT ANIMALS, COOKING WITH GRANDMA, ETC.)

IF THERE WERE SOMETHING ON TV THAT YOU THOUGHT I SHOULD SEE, WHAT KIND OF SHOW OR THING WOULD IT BE?

WHAT SPECIAL TALENTS DO YOU THINK I HAVE?
(FOR EXAMPLE, WORKING WITH PEOPLE, GETTING ALONG WITH CHILDREN, ART, MUSIC, MECHANICS...)

DID YOU EVER SAY TO ANYONE REGARDING ME, "DON'T YOU THINK SHE'D MAKE A GOOD _____ WHEN SHE GROWS UP?" WHAT WAS IT? HAVE YOU EVER THOUGHT ABOUT WHAT I'D BE HAPPY DOING?

WHAT AREAS OR CAREERS WOULD YOU SUGGEST I THINK ABOUT?

WHERE DO YOU THINK I SHOULD GO TO GET THE TRAINING (OR EDUCATION)?

Journaling—
This Is What I'd Be,
If Nothing Stood in My Way

Thinking about what you want to be or do when you grow up can be confusing and sometimes disheartening, can't it? Here is a little game that reveals a great deal about what you want for yourself deep in your heart.

You've just heard what others think about your talents and special abilities, and maybe you were impressed...or amused. But what do you, my strong and fearless Initiate, want for yourself?

Think about your future occupation and imagine that there are no obstacles at all, nothing to stop you from having what you want, absolutely no one in your way, no money problems, no education barriers—nothing can stop you. Okay?

So what's the scoop? What would you really do if nothing stood in your way?

Ha! I knew you'd have an answer right away. Good girl. That came from your heart. Now, all you have to do is make it happen—and hang all the obstacles. Hey! What's a few road bumps to a travel warrior like you?

Go for it.

chapter 29

But C.C., I'm Sick of School!

Sorry. No sympathy here—none.

Training and learning are essential to a young woman on the Goddess Path. You owe it to yourself to be fabulous in every way. Not everyone should be a scholar, that's for sure—it would be a stuffy, boring Abred if that happened! But the ancient Celts emphasized the importance of targeted education, specialized training through apprenticeship, and lifelong learning as the cornerstones to becoming a strong, self-sufficient woman.

Remember the Long View we talked about earlier? Well, a good part of your future depends on your occupation, and getting a good job is directly linked to the education and training decisions you make right now. The Clan Mothers would say that if you turn your back on education, or take a pass on specialized training at this point in your beautiful life adventure then, frankly, your Long View picture isn't so bright.

Being totally brutal, if you don't have enough education, you are considered unskilled. That translates into yucky, low-wage jobs, and they are very often the worst jobs—tedious and physically exhausting. You don't want that if you can prevent it.

Education and training—the stuff available to you right now—are lifesavers. They make all the difference between a life of crummy drudgery and low expectations, or one of challenge and fulfillment. Between unhappiness and happiness, you choose. Plain and simple.

Even way back during the times of Celtic clans, if a young initiate agreed to some special training that highlighted her natural skills, and then worked very hard at attaining it, she could change her Long View (her real future) for the better. With preparation and training, an initiate could happily—and realistically—imagine herself as a woman of high tribal status with a profession that suited her. She'd enjoy all the sweet confidence and prosperity that would be due her as a contributing woman within the Clan.

Even though centuries have gone by, some things never change. Accept this fact: It is your job, right now, to lay the groundwork for your future happiness by staying in school and getting the preparation you need. You **do not** shrink from challenge when you walk the Goddess Path. No! You stretch yourself and work hard at meeting your full potential as a highly spiritual woman.

If you don't do it for yourself, then at least consider doing it for the divine and loving Goddess who dwells within your soul. You'll come to thank Her for that inspiration.

Choose Your Role in the Clan

If I'm right about some things not changing, then it should be fun to look at the real jobs and professions available to women in the Celtic clans who worshipped the Goddess. Why fun? Because you can choose which one you'd like to have as your job in the community. Most likely, you can find a similar modern profession by scanning the Internet. Do this with your friends. Here are just a few of the possibilities for women within the clan.

Choose three if you prefer, and number them in priority from 1 to 3. Is there a comparable job in our world today? It just might be the one for you.

Herbalist	**Sheepherder (tending sheep)**
Healer (doctor)	**Cattle herder (tending cattle)**
Surgeon	**Animal husband (breeder/vet)**
Weaver	**Potion Mother (tonic and potions)**
Judge	**Dye maker (chemist)**
Lawyer	**Tanner (leather designer/maker)**
Dresser (hair stylist)	**Costumer (clothing designer)**
Midwife	**Brew Mother (ale/beer/wine)**
Bard (poet, writer)	**Nurturer (child care professions)**
Potter	**Mead maker (honey wine)**
High Priestess	**Face painter (make up artist)**
Jeweler	**Chieftain (community leader)**
Songstress	**Warrior (fight for rights/freedoms)**

chapter 30

The Incredible Blessing of Making Mistakes

I want to leave you with a very important message from the Clan Mothers:

> YOUR MISTAKES, THE FUMBLES AND STUMBLES YOU MAKE ALONG YOUR LIFE PATH, ARE A GIFT TO YOU—A PERSONAL GIFT OF ENLIGHTENMENT AND LEARNING—EACH AND EVERY ONE.

Mistakes? You gotta be kidding!

I know it spins your head around, but it is the truth. The most important lesson taught by the wise Clan Mothers was to value your mistakes, your screw-ups, your major goofs, and to see them in a different light.

Instead of beating yourself up, as you probably do right now every time you make a mistake (big or small), start to appreciate the circumstances or events that led to the mistake. Study your reactions and evaluate the consequences of what happened. Consider them a big fat present for your soul. A lesson package chosen specifically for you.

You see, the Aunties taught their initiates that before we came to Abred, we sat with the Goddess and decided what we needed to learn this time. We chose all our own challenges. And how better to learn than by making a mistake, experiencing all the fallout, and vowing never—ever—to do that again?

You may have noticed that when you don't learn from a mistake, sure as shooting, you do it again almost the same way. This happens frequently to women where men are concerned. Sometimes it takes several disastrous relationships before a woman gets the message. Or it may even take an entire lifetime of grief before she wakes up and learns her special lesson. Sooner, of course, is always better.

So you're sorta off the hook. Mistakes are not only okay, they are essential components in your learning package. They are the stuff that pushes you to learn about the real you; to give up crying and to come back smiling from your errors; and to laugh delightedly after a lesson well and truly learned. Mistakes are sprinkled all along the entire Goddess Path, nudging you to greater knowledge of your own soul, of your own true self.

So, my terrific initiate, my wise Path-walker, there's my last little bit of Celtic wisdom—Mistakes rule! We could live without them, but we wouldn't learn a damn thing!

Journaling—
Turn Your Nightmares into Dreams

Learn the art of turning your worst nightmares into heavenly gifts from the Goddess. By doing so, you never have to make the same mistake twice.

Learning through reflection and journaling

Use this journal space to jot down a few words reminding you of some of your worst mistakes. (You don't need all the gory details, just enough to recall the incident.) And remember to treat this like a research project—it's just raw information—so the memories won't bum you out and get you down.

Now, think about what happened, like an overview. Write down what you think you learned and how, in the long run, you benefited from having made that oh-so-human error. Did you learn where to put (or not put) your trust? Or to consider other people's feelings more often? Or not to act a certain way just to "fit in"? What was the message? What did you need to learn from each "mistake" as you walked the Goddess Path?

ONE TERRIBLE MISTAKE I RECALL:
(YOU MAY USE CODE WORDS FOR CONFIDENTIALITY.)

WHAT I THINK I WAS MEANT TO LEARN FROM IT:

OTHER SMALLER LESSONS TAKEN FROM THE ENTIRE AWFUL EXPERIENCE:

HAS THAT MISTAKE, OR SOMETHING SIMILAR, HAPPENED AGAIN?

WHY DO YOU THINK IT DID—OR DIDN'T—HAPPEN AGAIN?

ARE YOU GLAD YOU LEARNED THOSE LESSONS?

Wave Bye-bye to C.C.—For Now

Wow! Haven't we traveled a long way together in a short time! I had to run just to keep up.

Hey, and you weren't even sure what Maiden Magick was all about back at the beginning, were you? Yet, you jumped right in—and now you've mastered it! It is yours forever. With lightning speed you went from a neophyte (beginner), to an apprentice in training, and then rose to the higher level of an initiate. You even initiated yourself, with reverence and dignity, into the Way of the Goddess. What an amazing young woman you are. Here's a warm hug!

I sincerely thank you for the honor of walking beside you. And I thank you for the opportunity to learn together, for a teacher always learns from a bright and eager student. I know you'll have many fine teachers and mentors along your life Path, who will be as thrilled to work with you as I was. Dear One, I wish you the best.

My fondest hope is that when you are a crone you, too, will have the chance to enjoy the thrill of watching a young woman, like yourself, as she strides forth with feisty Goddess confidence along her own beautiful Goddess Path. 'Tis a rare and precious sight.

Now, I must step off your Path and duck back into the tangled forest I call home.

BLESSED BE, MY MAGICKAL MAIDEN.

Bibliography

The following books were mentioned in the text:

Dunwich, Gerina. *Herbal Magick*. Franklin Lakes, N. J.: New Page Books, 2003.

Estes, Dr. Clarissa Pinkola. *Women Who Run With the Wolves.* New York: Ballantine Books, 1992.

Knight, Sirona. *Goddess Bless! Divine Affirmations, Prayers and Blessings.* Boston: Red Wheel/Weiser, 2002.

Sabrina, Lady. *Celebrating Wiccan Spirituality*. Franklin Lakes, N. J.: New Page Books, 2002.

———. *The Witch's Master Grimore*. Franklin Lakes, N. J.: New Page Books, 2001.

Telesco, Patricia. *A Witch's Beverages and Brews*. Franklin Lakes N. J.: New Page Books, 2001.

———. *Exploring Candle Magick*. Franklin Lakes, N. J.: New Page Books, 2001.

———. *Mastering Candle Magick*. Franklin Lakes N. J.: New Page Books, 2003.

Walker, Barbara G. *The Woman's Encyclopedia of Myths and Secrets*. San Francisco: Harper, 1983.

Worth, Valerie. *The Crone's Book of Words*. St. Paul, Minn.: Llewellyn, 1971.

Index

D

E

F

G

H

I

K

About the Author and Illustrator

C.C. Brondwin is a professional woman who has been honored as an award-winning documentary journalist in both print and broadcast, and who has served as a senior executive at two universities, one a women's institution. Brondwin was raised as a spiritualist in a Celtic family where ceremony and ritual, talismans and amulets, were a part of her daily life. Both her mother and grandmother were recognized diviners and mystics. These inherited women's gifts of "knowing" led Brondwin on a spiritual quest to discover the Celtic Goddess of her ethnic roots. She studied herbalism and homeopathic medicine and traveled to Britain to rediscover the power and dynamism of early Clan Mothers who worshipped the Mother Goddess as Briganntia, or Brigit. Her dream is to recreate a far-reaching network of spiritual elders to serve as Clan Mothers to young women today.

She lives in the sunny foothills of the Canadian Rockies with her husband, artist and editor, William Johnson and their Newfoundland dog, Zimba. Visit C.C.'s Website at *www.ccbrondwin.com.*

Christine Ahmad is a self-taught artist and an instructor in paper art. Born in England, her whimsical drawings are inspired by her delight of growing up with daily myths of little people. Christine lives in the countryside with her husband Mo, and their two adopted dogs, Philby and Sam. Her home and studio are snuggled in a cozy grove of trees with a glorious mountain view just outside C.C.'s hometown.